LIKE A LOCAL

Susie Dent is an independent editor and translator who appears regularly in *Countdown*'s 'dictionary corner'. She is the author of six editions of *The Language Report*, an annual guide to the new words and phrases that find their way into the English language.

SUSIE DENT

HOW TO TALK LIKE A LOCAL

FROM COCKNEY TO GEORDIE

arrow books

Published by Arrow Books 2011

2 4 6 8 10 9 7 5 3

Copyright © Susie Dent 2010

Susie Dent has asserted her right under the Copyright, Designs and Patents Act, 1988, to be identified
as the author of this work

First published in Great Britain in 2010 by
Random House Books
Random House, 20 Vauxhall Bridge Road,
London SW1V 2SA

www.rbooks.co.uk

Addresses for companies within The Random House Group Limited can be found at:
www.randomhouse.co.uk/offices.htm

The Random House Group Limited Reg. No. 954009

A CIP catalogue record for this book
is available from the British Library

ISBN 9780099514763

The Random House Group Limited supports The Forest Stewardship Council (FSC), the leading
international forest certification organisation. All our titles that are printed on Greenpeace approved
FSC certified paper carry the FSC logo. Our paper procurement policy can be found at
www.rbooks.co.uk/environment

Mixed Sources
Product group from well-managed
forests and other controlled sources
www.fsc.org Cert no. TT-COC-002139
© 1996 Forest Stewardship Council

Typeset by
SX Composing DTP, Rayleigh, Essex, SS6 7XF

Printed and bound in Great Britain by
CPI Bookmarque, Croydon, CR0 4TD

Contents

Introduction

When I first told friends that I was embarking on a project collecting British dialect, their first thought was often that I would meet a lot of lonely people. I confess I feared they might be right. The speakers whose gems I was looking for were sure to be the last ones standing, bearers of vanishing vocabularies that would never be replaced. For the word 'dialect' has become synonymous with decline, just as English, we are told, is destined to become monolithic, bland, and peppered with universal lines absorbed from TV and Internet chat rooms.

It has been one of the nicest surprises of my career to learn just how wrong we were. That English is far from losing its edge I already knew – its golden age may even lie ahead of us still – but I accepted without question that it was different for dialect. Like most people I know, I believed that our local vocabularies are being ironed out at the same electric pace as new words are being coined, and for a much bigger audience than a particular neighbourhood. That what we now have is a general lexicon from which everyone, north and south, young and old, draws for expression. What I've discovered in the course of writing this book is that dialect is alive, well, and kicking hard. It's just doing so in new and different ways.

Of course, thousands of beautiful and unmistakably local words are dying out; many have already done so. They are just as surely to be missed as the new are to be celebrated. For the most part they belonged to a world now lost to us – one populated with horse-drawn ploughs, dockers and cotton workers, collieries and tin-mines. The lexicons of these and other industries are still there if you look hard enough, but as the need for them diminishes, so do the aural snapshots of the life they once so brilliantly described. Yet, over the 1,500 years of English's history, it was ever thus – words have come and gone (and often come back again) throughout, but the footprints they leave remain as telling as ever.

That *new* dialect is being coined today was an exhilarating find – of all the surprises that the writing of this book gave me, that was the big one. But there were lots of other discoveries along the way. As a collector of new words on the margins of Standard English, I've long realised that slang prefers particular subjects: sex, money, drink and drugs being at the top of the list. And so it is, I've discovered, with dialect. Local vocabulary collects around certain themes in just the same way. Some of these themes are as you might expect: given the nature of dialect – which is often as personal as it is local – it is hardly surprising that members of a family attract a whole range of different epithets. The staples in life, too, are natural targets for home-grown expression: bread, hunger, putting on a brew, packed lunches – all are core parts of our daily routine. And, just like slang, the lexicon for drunkenness is vast.

If the themes around which our local words congregate are fewer than you might expect, they make up for it with the dazzling variety within them. The dialect waterfront may be narrow – it is a world that deals in the easily accessible and concrete rather than the abstract – but it is infinitely deep. And it tells us an awful lot about Britain, its past, present and its locals (all of us).

Take a stereotype about the British: that we are a pessimistic bunch. If the number of local words for *ugly* is anything to go by – and it far surpasses the number for *pretty* – then on this occasion the cliché may have nailed it. And so it probably follows that the widest dialectal variation for things connected to our health and our body dwell on the more unsavoury aspects: blisters, for example, or armpits, or the faintly animalistic act of panting. It may seem cruel too that English dialect has quite so many words for physical handicaps or misfortunes. Whether knock-kneed, pigeon-toed or splay-footed, you would be hard-pressed to find a place in Britain that didn't have a local name for it.

Food, too, is usually mentioned in the standard portrait of the British, and rarely without a raised eyebrow. In dialect, however, food has a special place. And rightly so. For all the mockery over the British palate, the variety of foods wrapped up in its history is reflected in a wealth of local words. For bread alone there are estimated to be hundreds of terms which all hold a special resonance (not to say flavour) up and down the land. Being hungry is a labourer's lot, and the lexicons for being famished for your snack or packed lunch are particularly full. In the same vein, if there is anything which defines Britain in the world's eyes more than English beer, it is probably tea-drinking. The nation's two potable obsessions come together in the idea of brewing tea: an act which is called dozens of things depending on where in Britain you want to put the kettle on.

The British may be a nation of shopkeepers, as the saying goes, but it seems we are also a lot of gossips. And the act of exchanging titbits of information about each other is another theme that, when it comes to dialect, knows few limits. It persists across the nation in a glorious collection of names. Among its local variants are **jangle** (Liverpool and North Wales), **jaffock** (Lancashire) and **pross** (Durham). In addition there is **chamrag** which probably links **cham**, from champ meaning 'to grind or chew', and **rag**, which as a noun means 'the tongue' and as a verb 'to talk', often teasingly. But my favourite must be **hawch**, a development of the standard **hawk** meaning 'to spit' and today a term that has been reborn in the home of clotted cream and jam teas – to me it sounds like making the noise of a full mouth whether with food or gossip.

These are but a few of the subjects which, travelling up and down Britain, you will find packed with local vocabulary – earthy, funny and full of the resonances of the accent they were born for. Not all of the words are old by any means – the young are mixing it up locally like the best of their ancestors. And this is why dialect survives – it is being taken up, reshaped and moved on by new generations of English-speakers who, contrary to rumour, can still distinguish between home and country.

The selection of words in the book are but a minuscule proportion of the vast array of local words from our past and present. They have been chosen for their colour, for the stories behind them, and for the representation they give of the regions that use them. To those who look up their favourite word and find it lacking, I apologise, but I hope that they will find some new treasures along the way.

I am often asked for my favourite of all the words I collected (and of the many I didn't, thanks to the wonderful Voices Project conducted by the BBC, and to the efforts of many, many more before me). The truth is it changes every time I look at the words in this book. Two of the most enduring ones, though, have to be Northamptonshire's **make a whim-wham for waterwheels** – to idle away your time by doing nothing at all, and East Anglia's **dardledumdue**, a daydreamer. These choices must say something about me, but they also, I think, hold within them everything that is so wonderful about dialect. They, more than any rival expression in standard English, are simply born for their task. So far I've come across only one other person in each county who uses them. In this case at least, I hope they won't be lonely for long.

SD

Acknowledgements

When I took on the writing of *How to Talk Like a Local*, I didn't know that I was a few weeks pregnant, and the deadlines I'd agreed with my editor seemed fine to me. As it turned out, my daughter knocked the stuffing out of our schedule and it is to Sophie Lazar's huge credit that she patiently extended my completion date on more than one occasion and with endless patience. It's Sophie to whom I probably owe my biggest thanks, for her support and for our regular head-bashing about how to get the best book out of the material I'd collected.

Two people in particular helped enormously with the research and facts underpinning this book. Jonathon Green, Britain's foremost chronicler of slang, contributed a great many of the dictionary's rich examples together with accounts of their history. And Andrew Ball's contributions to the vocabulary collected in dialect's central themes were painstakingly researched and wittily presented. I owe them both a lot of gratitude and free lunches.

Thanks to my trips to Leeds and Manchester to the *Countdown* studios, and to impromptu conversations with friends up and down the land whom I harnessed as consultants, I was able to sample the lexicons of many a town and village. Acquaintances of all ages invariably had strong memories of childhood sayings and family expressions. Matt Speddings, Mark Swallow, Elisabeth Atkins and Colin Murray were all particularly helpful.

My final set of thanks goes to two passionate chroniclers of dialect. Simon Elmes contributed the book's essays on individual dialects and their pronunciation, which followed on from *Talking for Britain*, his hugely important and readable account of the local vocabulary collected so comprehensively by the BBC's Voices Project. Voices itself followed, on a smaller scale, in the enormous footsteps of Harold Orton's Survey of English Dialects at the University of Leeds, and the continuing work going on there, now spearheaded by this country's leading dialectologist, Clive Upton. Having met and worked with Clive during my time at Oxford University Press, for whom he wrote some of the best books I published, I know that it was his unfaltering enthusiasm and passion for dialect that swung my decision to write this book. Compared to such ambitious and necessary ventures as these, this book is a drop in the ocean. But it took its inspiration from them.

Susie Dent
March 2010

ackers

money (UK-wide but originally London)

Coming up with synonyms for money must be one of language's most consistent preoccupations. There are literally hundreds, of which the majority are slang. One traditional source has always been foreign travel, especially when laden by a tin hat, pack, rifle and ammunition, on the way to war. Whatever else the troops may bring back as souvenirs, it seems that the veteran's rucksack is also bulging with foreign cash, thus terms for money have included **piastres**, **kopecks**, **dineros**, **ducats** and many more. The **dollar**, after all, meant five shillings not all that long ago. Which is where **ackers** come in, which began their English-speaking life in the First World War and the allied campaigns in the Middle East. The *akka* was an Egyptian piastre; it worked in Cairo, and, when packed up and brought back home, it would work for Cockneys too – if only as a word.

See MONEY TALKS – OR DOES IT?, p. 144, *and also* GELT, MORGS, REVITS, SPONDULICKS

addle-headed

silly (chiefly central southern England)

Addle was an Anglo-Saxon word meaning 'stinking urine or other foul, stagnant liquid'. By the fourteenth century, it was commonly used as an adjective describing a rotten or putrid egg, and by the seventeenth referred to a person's brains, as **addled** (which has also been widely recorded in the south-west Midlands with this same sense of being silly or foolish). It was in the seventeenth century too that **addle-headed** first appeared. It still has wide currency across a whole swathe of the country, from Cornwall to the East Riding of Yorkshire, but it is probably in Wiltshire, Sussex and Berkshire that it is most entrenched.

See DON'T BE DAFT, *p.89, and also* BARMY, DAFT, FOND, GORMLESS, QUILT, SOFT

antwacky
old-fashioned (Merseyside)

Unlike such favourites as **fab** and **gear**, which delineate a Merseyside heritage as much as the Fab Four who allegedly used them, **antwacky** ranks a little less conspicuously on the local totem pole. But it is still to be heard there, where it means 'out of date' or 'unfashionable'. For all the lexicographical suggestions that have been made for it, it most probably comes from the local pronunciation of 'antique'.

See also DAGGY, SQUARE

apple-catchers
outsized knickers (Herefordshire)

Apple-catchers are the local equivalent of Bridget Jones's 'big pants'. They are, in other words, so big that they could be put to use during the harvesting of apples.

April gawby
April Fool (north-west Midlands)

Gawby is a simple substitution for fool, and today **April gawby** is restricted chiefly to Cheshire and Staffordshire although you may still find it in pockets across the Midlands and the North. **April gobby**, and the shortened **April gob**, are also to be found. Sadly for

A pinch and a punch

In 1957 winter was mild and spring came early, and so it happened that on 1 April that year, Richard Dimbleby, the BBC's senior current affairs broadcaster, was able to report from Ticino in Switzerland on the early – and bumper – spaghetti crop. Many intrigued viewers got in touch with the BBC, wanting to know how they might go about acquiring their own spaghetti bush. They had, of course, been duped by an April Fool which has entered British media lore. But, in the north of England and Scotland, they might have been the victims of an **April noddy**, or an **April gowk**, or a **huntigowk**, or even a **fool gowk**. In Lancashire, they could even have been the butt of a **niddy-noddy**.

The April Fool tradition arrived in Britain from Continental Europe during the seventeenth century – frustratingly, though, no one quite knows how it began. The term **April Fool**, meaning the victim of a trick or hoax played on the first of April, is first recorded in the 1690s, and the phrase **April Fool's Day** (as well as the variant **All Fool's Day**) is recorded shortly afterwards. The meaning 'trick or hoax played on this day' is not recorded until the middle of the nineteenth century.

From the late eighteenth century, an increasingly elaborate range of regional alternatives are recorded. This is typical of dialect words: the interest in regional language grew apace in the nineteenth century, partly out of a sense that the regional identities of Britain were slowly fading as the rural lifestyle underlying them dwindled away, and partly as a result of the vogue for philological studies which was sweeping the institutions of higher education throughout Europe. Indeed, quaint rustic customs (with odd names) were exactly the kind of thing to take the fancy of the Oxbridge-educated parsons who wrote many of the regional glossaries published at this time. What is notable about April Fool words is the extent to which they are confined to northern areas, with the ordinary term seemingly unchallenged throughout the South and most of the Midlands.

See also APRIL GAWBY, APRIL GOWK, APRIL NODDY, FOOL GOWK, HUNTIGOWK, MAY GOSLING

such a ripe-sounding word, the origins of all of these are unclear, although there may be a link with gape or gawp and hence the idea of an open-mouthed simpleton or fool.

See A PINCH AND A PUNCH, p. 3, *and also* APRIL GOWK, APRIL NODDY, FOOL GOWK, HUNTIGOWK, MAY GOSLING

April gowk

April Fool (Scotland and north of England)

Gowk derives from the Old Scandinavian word *gaukr* meaning 'cuckoo', and it is recorded in the medieval period with that same meaning in northern England and Scotland. At the end of the sixteenth century, an extended use of 'fool' or 'simpleton' began to emerge in Scots, from where it spread to the very north of England. As a result, **April gowk** became the natural variant of **April Fool** in that region.

See A PINCH AND A PUNCH, p. 3, *and also* APRIL GAWBY, APRIL NODDY, FOOL GOWK, HUNTIGOWK, MAY GOSLING

April noddy

April Fool (Lancashire, Cumbria and North Yorkshire)

Noddy is an old word for a fool or simpleton, first recorded in the sixteenth century. It is now practically obsolete except as it survives in **April noddy**. The phrase is recorded in a number of rhymes to be said to the victim of an April Fool, such as 'April-noddy's past an' gone, An' thou's a noddy for thinkin' on.' In Lancashire you can also find possibly the best variant of all: the beautifully alliterative and affectionate **niddy-noddy**.

See also A PINCH AND A PUNCH, p. 3, *and also* APRIL GAWBY, APRIL GOWK, FOOL GOWK, HUNTIGOWK, MAY GOSLING

arney

bad-tempered (Sussex)

> **Arney** means 'in a bad temper', 'contrary' or 'cantankerous' and is
> one of a variety of alternative spellings of 'ordinary' (*see* **ornery**).
> That ordinary should mean 'ill-tempered' seems to have been based
> on class. Ordinary in standard English may mean 'of the usual kind',
> but since the sixteenth century there has been a strong under-
> pinning of a low social order and of being 'not up to scratch'. From
> this sense of social inferiority comes arney, referring originally to the
> alleged coarseness and ill-temper of those of so-called lower rank. It
> probably follows that **arnary** or **orbnary**, (or **ommery**) cheese is
> still a label for a second-rate product, made from skimmed milk.

atweenhauns

now and again (Scotland)

> You have, as is so often the case with dialect, to say it out loud, and
> **atweenhauns**, so odd on the page, becomes, pretty much,
> 'between hands'. It means 'at intervals', 'now and again' or 'in the
> meantime'. The term is linked to Glasgow, but it is in general use in
> Scotland. Quite what type of hands remains a mystery. A figurative
> space lies, of course, between the human variety, but it's hard,
> looking at such phrases as Ayrshire's 'Atweenhaus make up the
> balance sheet', to resist the thought that there might just be a hint
> of something to do with cards, or perhaps the intervals of time
> between the hands of a clock.

auld shanky

death (Scotland and UK-wide)

> There have many images of death throughout history, and
> references to Death's age are a pretty constant theme, together
> with his traditionally skeletal physique. Hence **auld shanky**, in
> which auld is the Scots pronunciation of the standard 'old', and

shanky is his legs – a word which comes from the same place as the term **Shank's Pony**, an expression for the legs (where the 'pony' transport is in fact your own legs).

babby

baby (chiefly the North)

Representing a regional pronunciation of baby with a short 'a', **babby** is recorded in Scotland and in the north of England as far south as Derbyshire. As with **chiel**, this characteristically northern formation is also found in the South-West, but whether this is by chance or some other reason we may never know. The shorter form, **bab**, is also found, chiefly in Lancashire and West Yorkshire.

See SMALL TALK, p. 228, *and also* BAIRN, CHIEL, WEAN

backy, backie

riding pillion on a bike (UK-wide but particularly common in the North-East)

Backy, like **croggy**, has become a common term for riding pillion across Britain and is found particularly in Newcastle and the North-East. Other terms include riding **dinky**, **seatie** and **piggy**.

Pillion is one of the earliest words to have entered English from Gaelic, where it meant a small cushion, but for its absolute beginning we need to look to Latin and the word *pellis*, meaning 'skin'. The first people to ride pillion were on horses, not motorbikes or pushbikes, and they were not necessarily sharing the same mount, for in the fifteenth century a pillion was a light saddle, especially one used by women, and was made of fur or animal hide.

The sense of the seat behind a motorcyclist or cyclist dates back to the late nineteenth century. While pillion sounds rather formal, though, **backie**, and the other local variants for what we all do as children, says it so much better.

See also CROGGY

bag

to take a packed lunch (Yorkshire and Lancashire)

Taking a packed lunch, whether to work or school, has no geographical limits, but it has inspired a number of dialect terms. **Bagging** gets straight to the point: it means 'to take or carry a bag'. It's as simple as that.

See CLOCKING UP YOUR CROUSTS, p. 214, *and also* BAIT, CLOCKING, JACKBIT, NUMMIT, SNAP, TOMMY

bairn

baby; child (Scotland and north of England)

Like child, **bairn** has been a part of the English language since Anglo-Saxon times. Indeed, its first appearance is in the greatest work of Anglo-Saxon literature, *Beowulf*. Its linguistic roots are even deeper than that though, as parallel forms (or 'cognates') are found throughout the languages of the Germanic group, such as Frisian, German, Icelandic and even Gothic. By the medieval period, bairn was strongly associated with the North, a fact probably reinforced by Scandinavian versions of the word that arrived with the Vikings. In the *English Dialect Dictionary* (1901), it is recorded in Scotland, across the northern counties of England, and down into the East Midland counties which formed a core area of Viking power, such as Derbyshire and Lincolnshire. Over the course of the twentieth century, however, the word has become more and more restricted to Scotland and to the very north of England.

See SMALL TALK, p. 228, *and also* BABBY, CHIEL, WEAN

bait

food; a light snack (many areas but particularly Northumberland, Durham and Sussex)

> **Bait**, a term much used in the collieries in the nineteenth century, began life as far back as 1300 when it meant 'an attractive morsel of food placed on a hook or in a trap, in order to allure fish or other animals to seize it and be thereby captured' (*Oxford English Dictionary*). From there it developed, by the mid-sixteenth century, into meaning 'food' or 'refreshment', particularly as offered to horses or as a snack for travellers, and typically eaten between meals. Its origins seem to mix two meanings of the Old Norse *beita*: the first being to cause to bite; the second being food, especially as used to entice a prey – a meaning which of course lives on today.
>
> *See* CLOCKING UP YOUR CROUSTS, p. 214, *and also* BAG, CLOCKING, JACKBIT, NUMMIT, SNAP, TOMMY

Bandy-Ann Day

leftovers day (Sussex)

> If you're in Sussex and it's Monday you might well call it **Bandy-Ann Day**, where fellow locals would understand that as a consequence meals would consist only of leftovers. The name is intriguing: was there perhaps a Bandy Ann, some hapless housewife condemned to scraping out the weekend's pots for Monday's supper? It would be nice to think so, although it might be worth noting the Cumberland dialect word **bandylan**, a term for a woman of bad character, an outcast, a virago. Could it be that in less enlightened times a woman who failed to serve fresh food was simply equated with a bandylan?

bange

drizzle (Essex)

> It isn't common for an English regional word to be a direct borrowing from French, but that is what **bange** appears to be. Pronounced 'bendj', it derives from *baigner*, meaning 'to bathe, to wet'. It is one

of a number of 'drizzle' words found in East Anglia in the nineteenth century with the same basic form; others include **dinge** and **minge**. First recorded in 1790, much earlier than the others, **bange** is also the only one recorded in the twentieth century, and appears to be the core word of the group, with the others likely to be alterations of it, perhaps under the influence of words like damp and mist.

See DON'T TALK DRIZZLE, below, *and also* HADDER, MIZZLE, SMIRR

Don't talk drizzle

The weather provides possibly the greatest urban myth in linguistics history; that one about the Eskimos and their huge number of words for snow. Unsurprisingly, the Eskimos do have several words for snow, perhaps even a dozen or so, but the other ten, twenty or more popularly claimed for them are just illusory: Scotch mist if you like.

Scotch mist is now almost entirely used as a figurative expression, but until fairly recently it remained in literal use in Northumberland to refer to light rain or drizzle. Perhaps this isn't so surprising given that the lands either side of the England–Scotland border, up to the Highlands on one side and down through the Pennines on the other, have been so productive of words to describe this kind of rain. There are over forty words defined as 'to drizzle' in the English Dialect Dictionary, of which less than a quarter hail from south of Derbyshire and Nottinghamshire (and nearly all of those are from East Anglia, a statistic which tallies with the decision by the Victorians to make the South-West their pre-eminent holiday destination!).

All of which is before we take into account the already sizeable list of synonyms in more general use, such as spit, spot, speck, pick, sprinkle and drizzle itself. Then there is **dank** in north Lancashire, **dawk** in Scotland, **deg** in Northumberland (a variant of the obsolete **dag**), **damping** in the Midlands, **dozzle** in Cheshire, **haze** and **wet** in the North, **mist** in Kent and **smither** in Suffolk.

So, the next time anyone tells you how many words the Eskimos have for snow, talk to them about drizzle, and give them the list.

See also BANGE, HADDER, MIZZLE, SMIRR

---

bap

bread roll (originally Scottish; now general)

> The Scots invented the bap. In 1643, a baker of Dundee is recorded as engaged 'in beakinge of bunnes . . . kaikis and bappis to the tawernis' (i.e. in baking buns, cakes and baps for taverns). By the nineteenth century, the word had spread to the north of Ireland and the north of England, and it continued its southward progress, so that by 1975 *The Times* could use **bap** as a generally understood term in explaining what a **stotty** was: 'a local version of a bap, split and filled with meat or cheese'. It is still the case, though, that the word is more commonly used in the area starting in the Midlands and heading north.

> *See* OUR DAILY BREAD, p. 49, *and also* BARM CAKE, BUTTY, COB, MANSHON, NUBBIES, STOTTY

barm cake

bread roll (northern England)

> While **barm cake** is undoubtedly of northern usage, its life began in Cornwall, the most southerly part of Britain. **Barm** is an old Anglo-Saxon word for yeast, and the original Cornish use referred to a cake made with yeast, as opposed to an unleavened **heavy cake**. Somehow, in the early years of the twentieth century, the barm cake made a winding journey north and became another of the many northern words for a bread roll, **bap** or **cob**. It is now most commonly associated with Lancashire, where its application has been extended to people and to mean 'mad person, nutter', by association with the adjective **barmy**.

> Barm incidentally has also given us **barm-ball**, a light pudding or dumpling made of flour, a **barm-feast**, a yearly entertainment given in an alehouse, and **barm-head** and **barm-stick**, both meaning a 'soft-headed or foolish person'.

> *See* OUR DAILY BREAD, p. 49, *and also* BAP, BUTTY, COB, MANSHON, NUBBIES, STOTTY

barmpot

a slow-witted person (Lancashire and Yorkshire)

> The **barm** is the froth that forms on the top of fermenting malt
> liquors, or on a head of beer. A **barmpot**, or alternatively a
> **barmfly**, **barm-stick** or **barm-man**, is someone of feeble mind. A
> study of Pentonville prison from 1963 included the observation
> 'Thus a harmless schizophrenic will be classified by the staff as a
> "barmpot" and by the prisoners as a "nutter".'
>
> *See also* BARMY

barmy

silly (North and Midlands, South-East)

> **Barmy** is recorded by the 1950s Survey of English Dialects in two
> distinct areas: first in the North and Midlands, where it is the
> principal alternative to **daft** (in Lincolnshire and on Humberside it
> was the predominant choice), and secondly in the South-East from
> Oxfordshire across to East Anglia and down to Kent. It originally
> referred to **barm**, the yeast that creates the froth on beer,
> metaphorically suggesting a silly person was as insubstantial as the
> head on a pint. In English prisons, inmates would sometimes feign
> madness by 'putting on the barmy stick', i.e. by frothing at the
> mouth or, if you like, appearing full of ferment.
>
> *See also* DON'T BE DAFT, p. 89, *and also* ADDLE-HEADED, DAFT, FOND,
> GORMLESS, QUILT, SOFT

barri

excellent (Scotland)

> **Barry** or **barri** means 'excellent' or 'first-class' in Scotland, and
> should not be confused with **barra** – which is a Glasgow term that,
> according to Mike Munro's guide to modern Glaswegian *The
> Patter*, is used in phrases such as 'that's right inty ma barra', the
> city's equivalent of 'that's right up my street'. 'That' in this case may

well be categorised as barri or wonderful, but sadly we have little knowledge of where that one originates. The prevailing theory is that it is traveller talk, although frustratingly the word does not seem to be listed in any Romany dictionary.

barring-out
a method of school-pupil rebellion (Birmingham)

You may not find it going on today, but older generations of Birmingham families will still remember talk from their own parents of **barring-out**, a custom which involved shutting teachers out of the school classroom and demanding the day be declared a holiday. The result was often pandemonium. As Jonathan Swift put it in one of his journals: 'Not school-boys at a barring-out Rais'd ever such incessant rout.'

bawson
a fat or impertinent person (Yorkshire and northern England)

The **bawson**, or **bauson**, is a badger. It takes its root from the now archaic word **bausond**, an adjective meaning 'piebald' or, of an animal, having a white patch on its forehead. It may seem a strange leap from this neutral fact to a pejorative term for a fat or stubborn person, but animals have long inspired allusion and in this case the idea comes from the fatness and stolidness of the badger before its winter hibernation.

beat the devil round the gooseberry bush
to drag something out (Sussex)

'He did not think,' records one mid-nineteenth-century writer of an ageing parishioner, 'that the new curate was much of a hand in the pulpit, he did beat the devil round the gooseberry-bush so.' As recorded in Apperson's still authoritative *Dictionary of English*

Proverbs (1929), the devil takes up some 16 columns, twice that of God. And the concept of beating or whipping the evil one seems to have spread across the English-speaking world. By the look of things, however, the origin of this phrase seems to lie in America. There we find **beat** or **whip the devil round the meeting-house**, as well as **round the stump**, the first use of which is found in Virginia in 1786. Despite the ecclesiastical context of the quotation, anyone, not just curates, could do it. It means to be evasive, to ramble on without getting to the point, or – more deviously – to accomplish something by subterfuge. The image presumably reflects the fact that while the devil may be pursued and even punished, he is never actually caught.

beaut

an idiot (Liverpool)

Beaut would appear, whether from Liverpudlian or other lips, to be an abbreviation of beauty and/or beautiful, and to be used in a strictly ironical sense, reminiscent of the far older **natural**, which similarly used to denote a fool or something quite antithetical. The other primary users of beaut as a noun are Australians, where it ranks with **cobber** as one of the nation's linguistic badges. It may be that there is an Irish link – Liverpool has a large Irish community and of course early Australia had a heavy concentration of Irish immigrants (voluntary or otherwise).

beck

stream, rivulet (the North)

Beck is more or less the standard northern word for a stream. Like many such words, it is of Scandinavian origin. It is first recorded in the fourteenth century within those areas of England where Scandinavian influence was strongest, and has continued in common use since. The word, however, is not generally found as far north as Northumberland, where the Scottish **burn** is used.

See WATER WATER EVERYWHERE, p. 170, *and also* BURN, NAILBOURN, PRILL, RINDLE, SIKE, STELL

A twank and a wallop

Words that mean 'to hit' in its broadest sense are pretty common throughout Britain. Whacking, thumping, smacking, punching and clobbering are things we all do. Some of us may **twat** something (a word that is restricted only by register and not by region). Batter and clout may be slightly more common in the North but they too can be found up and down the land. There is one specific type of hitting, however, which shows both considerable regional variation and purely local vocabulary. That is, unfortunately, the hitting or beating of children as a punishment. Naughty children can be **toused** in Somerset, **jarted** in Yorkshire or given a good **bannicking** in Surrey.

In fact, they could be given a different type of beating pretty much everywhere. The verbs of spanking include **bash**, **baste** and **bray** in the north of England, **cane** in Essex, **clanch** and **clatch** in South Wales, **clout** and **dad** in Northumberland, **dust** in Surrey, **fettle** in Yorkshire and Staffordshire, **flop** in Lincolnshire, **hazel**, **hide**, **lowk** and **yuck** in Yorkshire, **hole** in Cumbria, **lace** in Northumberland, **larrup** in London, **leather** in the North-West, **lick** in the North, **scutch** in the Isle of Man, **skelp** in Cumbria, **slap** and **tancel** in Staffordshire and East Wales, **wale** in Derbyshire and **yark** in Northumberland.

Wallop, by the way, has been in general colloquial use since the early 1800s. It first entered the English language in the fourteenth century meaning 'to gallop' and derives from a variant of the French *galoper* found in northern France in the Middle Ages.

Of course, thankfully not so much hitting of children goes on now. But perhaps dialectologists of the twenty-second century will be researching regional variation in words for 'naughty step'.

See also BENSIL, MOLLYCRUSH, THRAPE, TWANK

bee nor baw

silent (Scotland)

> To say neither **bee nor baw** is to say nothing. Since neither term
> appears to have any relevant meaning of its own, perhaps the
> phrase is simply echoic, and a pair of words beginning with 'b'
> were chosen as a generic term for the unspoken words. Whatever
> its origins, it – ironically perhaps – certainly trips off the tongue.

bensil

to hit, beat (Yorkshire and Lincolnshire)

> Recorded in 1674 in the earliest glossary of North Country words as
> meaning 'to bang or beat', by the nineteenth century **bensil** is well
> documented with reference to punishing a child, especially in
> Yorkshire. The noun **bensilling**, or its near equivalent, is possibly
> even more common, as in the following Yorkshire example: 'Tom
> gav his lad a good bencillin for stealin taties.' It probably derives
> from an Old Scandinavian word meaning 'tension, impetus'.
>
> *See* A TWANK AND A WALLOP, p. 15, *and also* THRAPE, TWANK, MOLLYCRUSH

best

to make up one's mind (Cornwall)

> The standard meaning of besting someone is to get the better of them,
> or, as the *Oxford English Dictionary* defines it, to 'get an advantage
> over, outdo; to outreach, outwit, circumvent'. However, the Cornish
> verb **best** means something quite different, namely 'to ponder' or 'to
> make up one's mind'. The best guess at its meaning is that it is simply a
> contraction of a phrase such as 'I'm going to make my best decision'.
>
> There is one more, very specific, use in Cornwall, as described in
> the *English Dialect Dictionary*: 'going to sea when the weather looks
> threatening, and cruising on the fishing ground without shooting the
> nets, to see whether the sky will clear or not.' To those who sit and
> ponder just that, best must be the most useful word of the lot.

birle

to pour tea (Cumbria)

Birle is an Anglo-Saxon word meaning 'to pour out'. It derives from a noun meaning 'one who pours drinks' or 'cupbearer', which is used as early as the Old English heroic epic poem *Beowulf*. Birle differs, therefore, from words in the South-West meaning to pour tea, such as **empt** and **hell**, in that it was associated right from the start with the pouring out of drinks. It mirrors those South-West variants, though, in being used more often of alcoholic drinks than of tea. Recorded in Scotland and across most of the North, it refers mainly to the pouring of beer and whisky, but in Cumbria at least, to tea as well.

See KETTLE'S ON, p. 185, *and also* EMPT, HELL, MASH, MASK, SCALD, SOAK, TEEM, WET

bizzies

the police (Midlands and UK-wide)

The police is another of those themes, like money, death and drugs, that generates hundreds of synonyms. And here are a couple. In America they were (and among old hippies probably still are) the **fuzz**. Why? Because they 'make a fuss'. In Liverpool they're **bizzies**. Why? Probably because they 'get busy'.

blaefummery

nonsense (Scotland)

Some words just seem born for their task, and the echoic **blaefummery**, a Scottish term for nonsense, is one of them. It is an extension of **blaflum** (or **bleflum** or **blaeflum**), meaning 'a deception, a hoax, nonsense or illusion'; as a verb it means 'to cajole or impose upon'. There seems to be no indisputable origin – **blae** means blue or livid (in colour, that is), but there may be a link to **flummery**, meaning flattery, empty talk or humbug, and which has the charm of having started off its life meaning food, made of oatmeal or of flour, milk and eggs.

bleb

blister (the North)

Originally a synonym for blob without being specific to any particular region, **bleb** was by the end of the nineteenth century a word which distinguished the North from the South, being recorded everywhere north of a line running from Shropshire to Norfolk through Warwickshire, Worcestershire, Bedfordshire, Huntingdonshire and Cambridgeshire. Today, it is largely restricted to Yorkshire. In the twentieth century, the word took on a particular scientific meaning in cytology, the study of cells and organisms, and means 'a swelling or protuberance on the surface of a cell'.

See THERE'S THE RUB, p. 84 *and also* BLISH, GALL

blethered

tired out, exhausted (Yorkshire)

Deriving from a verb meaning 'to be out of breath' or 'to make someone out of breath', **blethered** was originally to be found in Yorkshire, Leicestershire and Warwickshire: 'He hit me full in the chest and quite blethered me' is one early example. The lovely **bellowsed** in Somerset has a similar meaning.

See ALL PAGGERED AND POOTLED, p. 115, *and also* BUSHWHA, DIRT DEEN, JIGGERED, LAMPERED, MAGGLED, WABBIT

bletherskate

a talker of blatant nonsense (Scotland)

If **blethered** can mean tired, the verb **blether** (and **blather**) has another common meaning in dialect: to talk nonsense (and a lot of it at that). A blethering, blathering or blithering idiot is one who doesn't stop talking senseless rubbish: a **bletherskate**, in other words. The seventeenth-century Scottish song 'Maggie Lauder' was the first to record it in the line 'Jog on your gait, ye bletherskate'. It became a favourite ditty in the American camp during the War of Independence.

blish

blister (the North)

> A shortened form of blister, **blish** is recorded in Cumbria, parts of Durham and the North Riding of Yorkshire, while in Northumberland and most of Durham **blush** holds sway. **Plish** in Westmorland and possibly **flish** in the North Riding are other pithy examples.
>
> *See* THERE'S THE RUB, p. 84, *and also* BLEB, GALL

blood

friend (originally London but now UK-wide)

> In 1519, the playwright John Rastell included in his play *The Four Elements* the line 'I shall bring here another sort/of lusty bloods to make disport'. His words provide the first example in the *Oxford English Dictionary* of the use of **blood** to mean 'a hot spark, a man of fire'.
>
> Blood is popularly treated as the part of the body which is inherited: the blood of parents and children, and of the members of a family or race, is seen as being distinct from that of other families or races. Today's use of blood to denote a friend invokes the sense of the blood of brotherhood and kinship – an extension indeed of 'blood brother' and 'flesh and blood'.
>
> In the US, blood has been an affectionate term of address to a fellow black person since the 1960s. Its arrival in Britain is no surprise: Black American English has been one of the primary sources of slang since the Second World War.
>
> *See also* BREDREN, BUTTY, CATERCOUSIN, CHUCK, CLICK, CREW, HOMIE, MARRA, MUCKER, SORRY

blootered

drunk (Scotland)

> **Blooter** is an old Scots word, probably going back to the sixteenth century, and is still part of the core language of Scotland and Ulster

today. Like many roughly contemptuous and abusive words, it has encompassed a number of specific meanings, but the two salient ones are 'a fool, a blundering oaf' and 'a noisy incessant talker, a babbler'. Whichever of these meanings is chosen, the sense is always there that a drunk person acts like a blooter. One Glasgow publication from the 1990s informs us that 'you don't have to get blootered, stagger home on a late night bus and wake up with a half eaten kebab on your pillow to have a good night out'.

For all the word's history, it is surprising that **blootered** meaning 'drunk' is so recent: no record has so far been found of its existence before the 1970s.

See LIQUID LUNCHES, p. 70, *and also* DRUCKEN, DRUFFEN, FLUTHERED, MALLETED, PISHED, PUGGLED, SKIMMISHED, STOCIOUS

bobbins
rubbish; nonsense (Lancashire)

Given the Lancashire origins of this term, it probably began as a reference to the bobbins that were spindles used to wind and unwind thread or yarn in the county's great textile factories. The bobbin was presumably seen as something small and, when used, insignificant, and so to refer to something as **a load of old bobbins** is to say that it has no importance.

Lancashire also offers the parallel phrase **that's all bobbin-wining**, an all-purpose term of disparagement or ridicule which refers to the prosaic task of winding (and not, as it would be easy to think, to whining). All that said, it is possible that the modern **bobbins** is at least a euphemism for the coarser **bollocks**, which, while giving slang yet another word for the testicles, also refers to something that is rubbish or worthless (just that bit more forcefully).

bock
to mess up, dishevel (Devon and the South-West)

Devon's **bock** means to mess up, as in 'don't bock my hair'. Where it comes from is debatable, but there may well be a link to **boke**, to thrust at, or to push. (That said, boke is more usually found meaning 'to retch' or 'to vomit', and as such, like all those slang words such as **hughie** and **ralph**, reflect the sound that's being made.)

boco
a lot (Sussex)

Boco, meaning a large amount, came directly across the Channel as a shortening of France's *beaucoup* and, like it, means 'a lot, a great deal'. The journey was probably made with British soldiers fighting the First World War. Indeed *beaucoup*, in various forms, has remained popular among the military, especially in the US.

The term, equally spelt as **boocoo**, **boo-koo**, **booku** and occasionally extended playfully to such as **boocoodles**, was picked up by the US army infantrymen (the Doughboys) of 1917–18; after that it reappeared in the Second World War. It persisted into Korea and seems to have received its greatest boost in the Vietnam War of 1963–74, thanks to Vietnam having been a French colony and many Vietnamese speaking French rather than English. Another, earlier, US source was that nation's own South, notably the once-French state of Louisiana, where the term was used, particularly among the black population, for some time before the First World War.

boiling
a number; a crowd (Sussex and Somerset)

Boiling, usually found as 'the whole boiling (lot)', is one of those terms that slips happily between slang and dialect. It means a crowd, a group, a large number. The root lies in the standard noun 'boiling' in the sense of a decoction of many things (or a lot of one thing) being boiled. Its first use is recorded in 1837, when it was used in the novel *Dog-Fiend* by Captain Marryat: 'He may . . . whip the whole boiling of us off to the Indies.'

How To Talk Like ... a Scot

This is, of course, a title designed to brew fury in the heart of Highlander and Glaswegian alike, not to mention the denizens of Aberdeen; it is tantamount to offering the key to how to speak like a Brit, so vague and ill-defined is it. Scots is a branch of the English language which split off some eight centuries ago, and which has developed, I would maintain, into a more or less autonomous and very distinctive language. A language, note, not a dialect.

So, as with languages the world over, there are subordinate and diverse varieties of Scots, each with its separate identity, vocabulary and, naturally enough too, accent. The Billy Connolly rufty-tufty Glasgow talk, with its sinuous vowels, rasping 'r's and almost inherent aggression, is a far remove from the polite and twisted vowels of Dourech or Doric, the speech of Aberdeen and its immediate surroundings. Likewise, travel to the very north of the Scottish islands and cup an ear to Shetlandic, and you'll hear sounds and words that feel as though they've been freighted in from Scandinavia.

Out west, on the other hand, in the 'long island' stretching from Barra to Harris and Lewis via South and North Uist, the native speech is gentle and sibilant, with its roots planted in the Gaelic substrate that is their natural habitat.

So you need to take your pick. Let's start with Glasgow, and the sound of the great Scottish conurbation. Consonants are spat out aggressively, glottal stops ruthlessly made and vowels are gargled away from anything like standard pronunciation, so 'ow' (as in town and house) becomes lengthened to 'toon' and 'hoos'. The long 'ay' in day and pay switches to 'ee' – 'dee' and 'pee': 'Ye knawked yerr pan ooyt oll dee,' remembers an old-timer about the rough working conditions on the Clyde – 'You knocked your pan out [worked yourself to death] all day.' Meanwhile the long 'oo' that you hear in moody, soon and room is tightened to a sharp 'uy' sound not so far removed from the narrow French 'u' you hear in tu, thus moody is more like 'muydy', soon is 'suyn' and room 'ruym'.

The short 'i' in it, hit and bitter routinely in the urban accent of Glasgow becomes 'et', 'het', 'betterr'; so the shipyards on the Clyde are 'shepyarrds'. In urban Dundee, you'll hear a not dissimilar aggressive urban accent, though with some differences – longer vowels (can is 'caan') and 'r' routinely omitted in words like 'from' which, using the Scots term 'frae', there is pronounced 'fae': 'Ay wuz fae Fin'rae' ('I was from Fintry' – an area of the city of jute, jam and journalism).

Contrast, if you will, the gentle Gaelic-influenced sound of the Western Isles, where *with* is 'withh', a *rose* becomes a 'rohsse' and *houses*, 'houssess', together with a syntax that's modelled on – if not literally translated from – these men and women's native tongue. Here the tune is softer too, with a wistful sing-song quality that's absolutely distinctive. 'I feel the strong Gaelic roots we have,' said an old crofter, 'are firmly embedded in the soil right round about us. I think if theess stoune dykes could talk they would talk to me in Gaelic.'

The sound of Shetland, on the other hand, is quite a different affair. Shetlandic owes much to its origins in the old Norn language, itself derived from Old Norse, the Scandinavian root of so much of our Viking-based linguistic heritage. Shetlandic sounds just so different from any other Scots – or indeed English – accent that it's almost impossible to describe. It's a gentle sound, as all these non-urban accents are, but many of its vowels (though not all) have taken a very different path from elsewhere in Scotland. Long 'o' as in *old* hardens and opens up to 'ah' (*older* becomes 'aalder', *cold* is 'caalt' while very cold is 'brally caalt'). Long 'i' (as in *slightly*) is 'oi' ('sloitly defferent') and here they talk of 'dellin' taaties' (digging potatoes) and 'heuffin' [huffing] something away' (throwing).

And if you think these strange sounds are somehow the result of distance, then think again. Because not so very far from the border with the south, the people of Hawick (pronounced 'Hoick') have their very own accent which is again a thousand miles from Received Pronunciation. 'He's an awfie maan fi the golf . . .' says a man describing his friend's sporting enthusiasm; and when it comes to counting, this is what a dozen sounds like in this Borders town: 'Yin, twae, thry, fawerr, five, seeks, seven, ight, niyn, tehhn, ilevn, twaal . . .'.

In the old days, many Scots lived in a **close** (tenement alley) and had a **dunny** or **cludgie** (outside toilet). The local gossip or **clatterbags** would be full of stories of how so-and-so had got **blootered** (drunk) the previous night and **boaked** (threw up) all over the **bunker** (worktop) in the kitchen and turned the whole house into a **bourach** (tip or muddle). Time to **flit** (move house) perhaps? At school, the **dominie** (teacher) would **skelp** (smack) you on the **doup** or **erse** (backside), if you got into fights – '**I'll skelp your puss**' ('I'll smash your face in') would often be heard in the yard, unless you were **dogging off** (playing truant). A child would run **messages** (shopping) for her parents who were **knockin their pan out** (hard at work) all day.

Whoever said Scots wasn't a language?

SIMON ELMES

bonny

pretty (Scotland, Ireland and northern England)

> First recorded in Scotland in the sixteenth century, **bonny** is probably the earliest and most important of the words that began by meaning 'pretty' and then developed into adjectives of general approval meaning 'good, excellent'. It is common throughout the North and Midlands of England and is sporadically recorded further south. The Survey of English Dialects also collected the shortened form **bon** in Cheshire.

> *See* SITTING PRETTY, p. 77, *and also* FITTY-LOOKING

bosting

excellent, great (West Midlands)

> The term **bosting** (or simply **bostin**) is widely used throughout South Staffordshire and has become pretty much synonymous with Black Country dialect. Its general meaning is 'large in size'; pronounced with the local accent it is quickly linked to the idea of bursting or busting. More often though it is an all-purpose term of approval – and in this there may be a possible link too with 'boasting'. Whatever its origin, the term is clearly thriving, especially if the Baggies (West Bromwich Albion FC) have 'played a boster'!

> In Northern Ireland a similar term is **beezer**, meaning 'an impressive or large example of its kind', while that same word in Scotland is used of a smart person.

bowdy-legged

bow-legged (Yorkshire and Kent)

> **Bowdy-legged** is the creative solution in Yorkshire and Kent to the competing claims for supremacy of **bow-legged** and **bandy-legged**. In both areas, the pronunciation of the second part of the word is recorded as 'legd' rather than 'legid'.

> *See* STRAIGHT (OR NOT SO STRAIGHT) TALKING, overleaf

Straight (or not so straight) talking

Describing people with legs curving outwards at the knees is, for the most part, a tale of two words. **Bow-legged** appears at the beginning of the seventeenth century, and **bandy-legged** at the end. In both cases the early evidence for them is from translations of classical Latin works (by Ovid, Juvenal and others) in which they are used to translate the Latin word *valgus*. (There is also an isolated example of bow-legged meaning 'knock-kneed' in the sixteenth century in a Latin-to-English dictionary.) If both did indeed start life as standard words, then they have both remained so, although over time bow has become somewhat more common in standard English, and bandy rather more colloquial. If any regional tendency can be attached to either, it would be that bandy-legged is more common in the South-East.

Apart from in Somerset, where some of the people are **scrod-legged**, local words are all variations or elaborations on these two basic terms. There is, however, a notable regional variation in the pronunciations. Except in the South, the -legged part of bow-legged is practically always 'legd', whereas for bandy-legged, 'legid' is a common pronunciation throughout the country. As for *valgus*, it too has found its way into English as a technical term in orthopedics.

To add a bit of spice to the mix, you might be **bandy-kneed** in Shropshire, **bower-legged** in Cheshire, **bow-footed** in Northamptonshire, **straddly-bandy** in Kent, and in that unfortunate-sounding predicament of being scrod-legged in Somerset.

See also BOWDY-LEGGED

brassic

poor; broke (London and the South-East)

> This twentieth-century word is a corruption of 'boracic', short for boracic lint (a type of medical dressing made from surgical lint), which in turn is rhyming slang for skint. The *Oxford English*

Dictionary's first mention of **brassic** is from 1982 and an episode of the sitcom *Only Fools and Horses*: 'Oh no, come on, Del, most nobility are brassic nowadays aren't they?' While it is unlikely to have been coined for the series (there is evidence of its usage dating as far back as 1945), it was certainly popularised by it. Indeed, John Sullivan, the creator of the series, can be credited with popularising many more Cockney terms, including **plonker**, **dipstick** and **hooky** (gear). Perhaps the most successful of all was **luvvly jubbly**, which he took from an advertisement for an orange drink and subsequently propelled into the English language as slang for 'tickety boo' or great stuff.

More recently, brassic and **brassic lint** have drifted north of the border: Irvine Welsh's 1993 novel *Trainspotting* includes the line 'Every cat's dead palsy-walsy likesay, but once they suss that you're brassic lint, they sortay just drift away intae the shadows.'

bredren
friend or friends (UK-wide but particularly London)

If you are bang up to date, you might refer to your friends as your **bredren**, a Biblical allusion that is synonymous with **brer** (as in brother, and Brer Rabbit). The less-used female equivalent is **sistren**.

See also BLOOD, BUTTY, CATERCOUSIN, CHUCK, CLICK, CREW, HOMIE, MARRA, MUCKER, SORRY

buckle-beggar
a clergyman who performs irregular marriages (Scotland)

The **buckle-beggar** was, in the early eighteenth century, a literal buckler or joiner of beggars, with a beggar being someone who wanted or requested something that was usually frowned upon or forbidden in general society. He was the equivalent of the older **hedge-priest**, another clergyman who joined together those outside the norms of respectability: those who indeed might often be found quite literally living beneath or in a hedge.

The buckle-beggar's rather more romantic role was carried out at Gretna Green, where since 1753 it has been possible for young couples under the age of majority to be married without the usual licence and more importantly without the asking of the banns (the bit where interested – and outraged – parties can step forward and cry 'Stop!') before the wedding. The difference between English and Scottish law meant that anywhere in Scotland would have worked, given someone ready and willing to perform the necessary job, but Gretna Green was the first place runaway lovers would reach after crossing the border. In the event, the ceremony was originally performed by a blacksmith, since the law allowed any marriage, as long as a declaration was made in front of two witnesses. In Gretna Green the role was taken up by the village's two blacksmiths, who became otherwise known as **anvil priests**.

bummerskite

a lazy person or a drudge (Yorkshire)

Bummerskite manages to combine two opposing meanings in its three syllables: on the one hand it signifies a lazy person, on the other a hard-worked drudge. It consists of two words: **bummer**, a 'boaster, empty talker or idler' (although it can also mean something big, or a large example of something) and, pretty much saying the same thing again, **skite**: 'an opprobrious epithet for an unpleasant or conceited person; a meagre starved-looking ugly fellow' according to the *English Dialect Dictionary*. It is this latter definition, the meagre fellow, that presumably lies behind the sense of drudgery. Bummer crossed the Atlantic in the mid-nineteenth century and was used there to mean a lazybones; it is probably the root of America's **bum**, a tramp (properly **hobo**, a word for which no fixed origin has yet been established), although the lexicographer Schele De Vere suggested in *Americanisms* (1872) that 'he is, far more likely, descended from the German *Bummler*, a man who goes about without aim and purpose, and lives on the fruits of other people's labor'. Certainly bummer's first US outing in a newspaper of 1855 is in an unarguably German context: 'Come, clear out, you trunken loafer! Ve don't vant no bummers here!'

bunce

cash; gains (London)

> **Bunce** started off life among London's street greengrocers or costermongers (literally costard – a variety of apple – sellers) where it was spelt **bunts** and meant second-rate apples. These apples were sold off cheaply or even given away to market boys, who could in turn sell them at a small profit. Bunts were further divided into **fair bunts** and **unfair bunts**, depending on whether or not the coster was aware of his boy's tricks. Gradually the word became associated with the concept of a quick, easy profit, extras, bonuses and other sources of 'money for nothing'.

bunk off

to shirk responsibility (UK-wide but particularly Lincolnshire and Leicestershire)

> In his *Glossary of words used in the wapentakes of Manley and Corringham, Lincolnshire*, published in 1877 (**wapentakes** were subdivisions of certain English shires), Edward Peacock lists the word **bunk** as meaning 'to run away, to make off'. This is the *Oxford English Dictionary*'s first citation for the verb, while the slang chronicler Jonathon Green has found instances as early as the mid-nineteenth century, where it meant to escape or run off under pressure: a sense which remains with us today. At the close of the nineteenth century is evidence too of the verb **bunk about**, meaning to wander around.
>
> All such instances of bunk are fairly localised around the counties of Lincolnshire and Leicestershire. From around 1890, however, bunk took on the meaning of being expelled from school, a use

which seems geographically widespread, certainly in relation to public schools: the *OED* quotes it as slang from Wellington College in Berkshire and gives further examples from Rugby School. The earliest instance of bunk to mean wilful truancy on the part of the child seems to be 1949, where there are records of children 'bunking about' in the fields 'rather than working in class'. Today, of course, **bunking off** can be applied to any shirking of responsibility, and this more general sense may in fact have a longer history: it very likely spilled over into local slang long before 1949.

See BUNKING AND PLUNKING, p. 192, *and also* DOG, MITCH, NICK OFF, PLAY HOOKEY, PLUNK, SAG, SKIDGE, SKIVE, TWAG, WAG

burn

stream, rivulet (Scotland and Northumberland)

Burn is an Anglo-Saxon word with a range of watery meanings, such as 'spring', 'fountain' and 'river'. By the thirteenth century in Scotland and the Border region, the specific sense of a stream smaller than a river had arisen. It can frequently be seen as an element in place names, the most famous of which is perhaps Bannockburn, an area that remains the heartland of the word's use. It is now standard in Scotland and Northumberland and is also recorded in Cumbria and Durham. In the south of England, **bourne** represents a parallel development of the same original word.

See WATER WATER EVERYWHERE, p. 170, *and also* BECK, NAILBOURN, PRILL, RINDLE, SIKE, STELL

bushwha

exhausted (Liverpool)

Bushwa, spelt without the second 'h', is a euphemism for bullshit, and means 'rubbish or nonsense'. Add the 'h' and the word confusingly means something quite different. **Bushwha** is used in Liverpool to mean 'exhausted'; it comes from the synonymous US slang **bushwhacked**, a word based ultimately on the standard

The mirror cracked

There seems to be one significant difference between local dialect words and modern slang terms for ugly, and it is really a difference of context. Modern slang items – **butters**, **dobra**, **muntin**, **maftin**, **rough**, **duffy** – all refer originally to a woman's looks; they all mean 'sexually unattractive'. The same is true of nouns meaning 'an ugly person', such as **munter**, **minger**, **moose** and **dog**; they mean 'a sexually unattractive person'. By contrast, older dialect words have a wider scope. They typically overlap with foul, loathsome or unpleasant. When applied to people, they also tend to have some implication of untidiness or awkwardness rather than being applied solely to physical features. And they are at least as likely to be applied to men as to women.

English term **bushwhack** meaning 'to live in the backwoods'. The most literal meaning of bushwhacked is 'beaten'. As noted by the US writer Schele De Vere way back in 1872: 'Originally it was a harmless word, denoting simply the process of propelling a boat by pulling the bushes on the edges of the stream, or of beating them down with a scythe or a cudgel in order to open a way through a thicket.' It was that last meaning that became predominant. From there the term took on, particularly in slang and figurative meanings, the idea of ambushing or attacking without warning, but also of hiding something surreptitiously or borrowing without permission. The Liverpudlian use has more to do with the feeling of being whacked, as in beaten down by exhaustion, a word that shares a very similar history.

See ALL PAGGERED AND POOTLED, p. 115, *and also* BLETHERED, DIRT DEEN, JIGGERED, LAMPERED, MAGGLED, WABBIT

Some examples fitting this model include **agar** in Cornwall (from the Cornish **hager**, 'ugly, foul'), **burly** in Dorset (a survival of a Middle English word meaning 'stout, domineeringly big') and **rawley** in Orkney (possibly connected to the Norwegian *raal*, 'untidiness'). All of these words are now obsolete or vanishingly rare. Perhaps none of this is surprising, given that over the course of the past century or so, the 'sexually unattractive' sense of **ugly**, which once also meant 'frightful or horrible, through deformity or squalor' (as defined in the *Oxford English Dictionary*), has also become dominant compared to other senses of that word.

Outside of Scotland, **minging** has led the way for a whole host of new slang terms for ugly, including **dross**, **fusty**, **mingin**, **mong**, **monger**, **moose**, **rank** and **skank**. Not the most flattering picture of our current mores.

See also BUTTERS, DUFFY, FUSTY, LAIDLY, MINGING, MUNTER, OBZOCKY, RANK, SKANK

butters
ugly (UK-wide but particularly in London and Birmingham)

The use of the word **butters** to mean 'ugly' arrived in the US in the early 1990s, although it had been around pre-1970s with the different sense of naive, spoilt or foolish. There is most probably a link to the American **butt**, or buttocks, with a possible play on the term **cheesy** in its sense of second-rate or cheap and nasty. Paradoxically **butter**, often spelt **butta** (particularly in hip-hop lyrics) means attractive, of both a woman and a man – in this case suggesting the smoothness of the spread and the fact perhaps that they move through life like butter.

See THE MIRROR CRACKED, above, *and also* DUFFY, FUSTY, LAIDLY, MINGER, MUNTER, OBZOCKY, RANK, SKANK

butty
bread (UK-wide, particularly northern England)

As one might expect, a **butty** is a slice of bread and butter or one of bread spread with treacle, sugar or some other sweet topping. Yet while you might assume that the **buttycake** (or **buttercake**) would increase the sweetness to bread ratio, it is, in fact, nothing more exotic than simple bread and butter. This sense of butty, then, is a straightforward contraction of butter.

See OUR DAILY BREAD, p. 49, and *also* BAP, BARM CAKE, COB, MANSHON, NUBBIES, STOTTY

butty
a companion, a mate (the North-East)

The use of **butty** to mean 'a friend or workmate' dates back to the early nineteenth century. It probably comes from the noun **booty**, meaning 'gains' or 'prizes', and more particularly from the sixteenth-century phrase **to play booty**. To play booty with someone was to share their plunder as a confederate or a **booty fellow**.

A **butty** was traditionally a companion, and particularly a miner's mate or the middleman between the mine-owners and the workmen. **Butty-colliers** and **butty-gangs** are groups of men to whom a portion of the work in some large engineering enterprise is allotted, and who divide the proceeds equally among themselves.

See also BLOOD, BREDREN, CATERCOUSIN, CHUCK, CLICK, CREW, HOMIE, MARRA, MUCKER, SORRY

caffy-hearted

squeamish (northern England, particularly the North-East)

For a word that means unsaleable fish to make the jump from the market stall to the world of the emotions seems something of a stretch. But stretched it is, for **caffy**, also **chaffy**, comes from **caff/chaff**, a word that has meant 'the husks of oats' since the tenth century (and still does in the North and the Midlands). By extension caff became anything seen as worthless or figuratively light, including rotten or at least unsaleable fish, as well as rubbish of any kind. Finally we come to **caffy-hearted**, which followed this trail and which came to mean one whose heart is light – not in the sense of cheerful, but in that of lacking gravitas or weight. Hence the Teesside definition: 'squeamish'.

cag-mag

something worthless or rubbishy (Lancashire and Yorkshire)

Cag-mag began life in the eighteenth century as a term to describe a tough old goose, and from there came to mean 'unwholesome or even rotten meat'. In that pre-foodie world, such geese, which came from the North and Midlands (the word apparently first emerged in Lincolnshire) were frequently dumped on the undiscriminating London market. Today, the culinary uses seem to have disappeared but both dialect (as a 'gossip', a 'meddlesome old woman', a 'practical joke' or 'mischief', and as a verb, 'to nag') and slang (in the UK as 'rubbish' or 'odds and ends', and in Australia 'idle chatter') have kept the word alive and well.

All the local gossip

As befits an activity that we all spend so much time doing, there is an apparently unceasing list of words describing either the act of gossiping or a person who engages in it. In fact, very few of these lie outside of two main categories. First, there are those words that refer to the chatting or prattling on that is usually how gossip changes hands. These range from fairly obvious formations like **chatterbag** in the South-West, **gabber** in Berkshire and **natterer** in Sussex to the more colourful (and clearly related) **chamragging** in Wiltshire and **hamchammering** in Somerset. The second category is made up of words that refer to the function of gossip in exchanging news and information such as **newsing**, and **newsbagging**, which can still be found in the South-West. Examples with more explicitly negative connotations, such as **scandalmonger** in the South-East and **taler** in Dorset, could also be included here. Among those that don't fit these tendencies are **clonc** in west Wales, which is derived from the Welsh **cloncian**, 'to gossip', and the very odd but nice **gallivanter** in Cheshire.

And that's not all. There is **blatherskite** (Durham), **cag-mag** (Gloucestershire, Sussex), **call** (Yorkshire), **caller** (Yorkshire, Lincolnshire), **canter** (south-west Midlands), **chatterbox** (various bits

The origins of **cag-mag** remain unproven. The mid-nineteenth-century slang collector John Camden Hotten suggested a corruption of the Greek *kakos mageiros*, a 'bad cook', and attributed it to university slang. Most etymologists reluctantly say no to that, even if no alternative has surfaced, although there may be some connection between the dialect verb **cag**, meaning 'to gossip', and our standard verb cackle, whether as a goose or a human. We do know that a **mag** was once a gossip or a scold and was a shortening of magpie, a notorious chatterbox of a bird.

of the South), **chattermag** (South-West), **chopse** (Berkshire, Staffordshire, Gwent), **clat** (Lancashire), **clat-can** (Lancashire), **gad** (Yorkshire), **gallivanter** (Cheshire), **gasbag** (Berkshire, Shropshire), **houser** (Cornwall), **jaffock** (Lancashire), **housing** (Cornwall), **labbing** (South Wales), **magger** (Gloucestershire), **magging** (Yorkshire), **natter** (Oxfordshire), **nattering** (South, esp. South-East), **news-bag** (chiefly South-West), **news-canter** (Gloucestershire), **newser** (South-West), **newsmonger** (South, esp. South-West), **newsmongerer** (Devon), **newsmongering** (Somerset), **newspad** (Wiltshire), **nosey parker**, **rattlebox**, (chiefly South-East), **tattler** (Essex), **tick-tatting** (Norfolk), **tongue-wag** (Worcestershire), **yaddering** (Cumbria); **yapper** (Essex).

The very word 'gossip', by the way, has an interesting origin in itself. In Old English **godsib** was the word for a godparent. It meant, literally, 'a person related to one God', and came from **god** 'God' and **sib** a 'relative' (this still survives in the word sibling). Gossip came over time to be applied to a close friend, particularly a female one, who was invited to be present at the birth of a child. Linguistic evolution is a strange thing, for at some point that same woman took on the negative aspects of a newsmonger or tattler, indulging in light and trifling chatter.

See also CANK, CANT, CHAMRAG, CLISH-MA-CLAVER, COOSE, JAFFOCK, JANGLE, NEIGHBOUR, PROSS, TALE-PYET

cank

a gossip (the Midlands, chiefly south-west)

Formerly recorded as a verb throughout the Midlands (except Lincolnshire), **cank** has also been used as a noun (denoting both a person who gossips and the act of gossiping itself) chiefly in the south-western part of the region. It is still recorded in at least Warwickshire. The sense of idle chatter is an extension of a meaning of cank, recorded in the same region in the mid-eighteenth century, to mean the honking of a goose (chosen for its onomatopœia).

See ALL THE LOCAL GOSSIP, *above, and also* CANT, CHAMRAG, CLISH-MA-CLAVER, COOSE, JAFFOCK, JANGLE, NEIGHBOUR, PROSS, TALE-PYET

canny

nice; good (Northumbria)

> **Canny**, like its Scottish counterpart meaning 'sensible' or 'wise', may derive from the verb 'can'. It is used all over Northumbria as a multi-purpose intensifier, such as in the strange combination overheard in the conversation of local teenagers who declared a new download to be 'canny wicked' a phrase in which the language of two generations collide.

cant

a gossip (south-west Midlands and south-east Wales)

> **Cant** may be a variant of **cank** or simply an imitative formation in its own right. It typically occurs slightly further south-west than cank, and follows the same pattern of a noun deriving from an earlier verb and gradually becoming by far the most common form of it. **Canter** is also found in the south-west Midlands and **canting** in Newfoundland. That it crops up in Canada is not as surprising as it might appear, since the dialect of south-west England is one of the most important historic sources of Newfoundland English.

> *See* ALL THE LOCAL GOSSIP, p. 34, *and also* CANK, CHAMRAG, CLISH-MA-CLAVER, COOSE, JAFFOCK, JANGLE, NEIGHBOUR, PROSS, TALE-PYET

carsey

toilet; an unappealing place (London and now UK-wide)

> **Carsey**, otherwise spelt **carsi**, **cawsy**, **karsey**, **karzey**, **karzi**, **karzie**, **karzy**, **kazi**, **khazi** and **kharzi**, comes from the Italian *casa*, 'a place', and has meant 'a lavatory' since the late nineteenth century. Indeed, it means anywhere the speaker dislikes, whether a brothel or a thieves' den, or a place that may not literally be one, but that resembles a lavatory: in other words one that is messy, dirty and unappealing. About the only respite was around the 1880s

when for a while **carsey** meant just a house or pub, with no
negative overtones at all.

cat melodeon
terrible; appalling (Northern Ireland)

Surely to be ranked among the strangest of all dialect terms, **cat
melodeon** is an expression that in Northern Ireland immediately
rings alarm bells. For a term so colourful it is surprising – and hugely
frustrating – that its origin is so elusive. That hasn't stopped people
from trying, though. Among suggestions and local myths is the
supposed tendency of accordion (or melodeon) players to fluff their
notes, which can reproduce the terrible howling of a cat on heat.
An alternative, and perhaps more lexically feasible, theory links the
term to a slang use of **cat** to mean 'terrible' or 'shocking', or to the
Irish term **cat marbh** which means 'mischief' or 'calamity'. Finally,
there is a suggestion that the term may simply be an abbreviation of
the noun 'catastrophe'. Whichever of these it may be, or another as
yet uncovered, the term lives on as a vivid illustration of just how
vibrant dialect can be.

catchy
changeable (of weather) (Devon and the South-West)

To rush to the lavatory is to be 'caught short', and the kind of
weather that is **catchy**, at least in Devon, is the sort that will catch
you equally unawares, albeit this time in the middle of a field
without shelter. Catchy thus means that the weather is changeable,
usually showery, and **catching-time** is that wet season –
presumably that of April showers – in which people working in the
fields are caught by frequent downpours.

How to talk like... **a Scouser**

The sound of the Mersey is unlike any other in Britain. It's also perhaps the best-known British accent the world over as a result of a certain bunch of young musicians from Liverpool who made it big in the 1960s and whose relatively gentle and genteel variety of Scouse became a model for all young people to admire. As a result of the Beatles and others, the Mersey was no longer just a river, but *de MAIRzee*, across which you took a ferry. We learned too about Penny Lane and Strawberry Fields and became familiar with that drone-like tune of Liverpudlian English, with its curvy upward inflections and breathy word-ends.

For a British accent that attracted so much celebrity around the world (how often have you heard, say, a Bristol or a Birmingham voice making waves on the legendary American Ed Sullivan TV show as Scouse did when the Beatles visited in 1964?), it's surprising that the speech of Merseyside and Liverpool in particular regularly comes near the bottom in surveys of favourite British accents. It has its negative associations, of course, of lazy *scallies* on the fiddle, of dock strikes and dodgy town-hall deals. But today the sound of 2008's capital of culture should be riding high once more.

They say the term 'Scouse' derived from an old fisherman's stew called 'lobscouse' and that the term originated in Norway, but the accent has nothing of the fiords to it and owes much of its bedrock to the Irish speech of the area's many settlers from the west. Very different too, this Liverpool speech, from the sound of 'Lanky' talk, the accent of Lancashire in which county Liverpool nominally finds itself, but with which it has little or nothing in common in terms of accent. Only on the Mersey do you hear those trailing ends-of-words with hard consonants like 'k' and 'g' that sound as though the speaker's got a mouthful of phlegm. Here a *book* becomes a 'booCH' (with the final sound like a Scottish *loch*), *crack* (as in 'good crack' or fun, from the Irish *craic*) is 'crACH', and that supposedly routine Liverpool tag, *wack*, for a bloke (from Gaelic *mhac*) comes out as 'waCH'.

And still listening closely to the way a Liverpudlian ends his words, unless you're familiar with it, the fade-away to a hiatus that you hear as he pauses to consider the rest of his utterance: 'but . . .' which trails off to 'booohh . . . on the oother hand . . .' comes as a surprise. Likewise, that familiar Mersey *lad* becomes for locals a 'laahh', and words ending in 't' also soften towards a 'th' sound (*fit* becomes 'fith . . .').

And Liverpool's idiosyncratic vowels are typically among the really distinctive British accents, a complete shift-around from Received Pronunciation. So, *burn* sounds like 'bairn' and, as I've mentioned, the *Mersey* is the 'mairzee'. On the other hand, that very sound 'air' that normally turns up in *pair*, *dare* and *care* becomes in the mouth of a Scouser 'urr'; thus 'purr', 'durr' and 'curr'. The short 'o' vowel that crops up in words like *horrible* and *lot of* can harshen towards 'harrible' and 'larra', while long 'u' is famously never 'oo' (as in *school*) but 'yew'. So the city's very name is 'Liverpyule', where the Beatles went to 'skyule' and later wrote the 'The Fyule on the Hill'.

The consonant 'r' is quite pronounced – *verbal* is 'vairrbal' – but where in other parts of the country (particularly the South-West and in the rest of Lancashire) there is strong rhoticity, or r-sounding ('haRRk that baRRk!'), in Liverpool it's not sounded at all. But perhaps the most surprising and indelibly Scouse vowel is the regular tendency to turn the long 'o' sound (in *phone*, *home* and *rolled gold*) into something that sounds suddenly very posh. So you can be listening to the 'rolling gales of Mersey' dialect pouring forth in your average Birkenhead boozer and suddenly it lurches into something straight out of a cut-glass elocution lesson, as that 'o' becomes the triphthong (three-sound) 'eyo'. So a conversation about bling, say, that asserted that someone had *a rolled gold phone at home* would sound something akin to 'reolled geold pheone at heome'. You'd hardly credit it, wack!

So there was this **scally** (reprobate), see, who was **sagging skewl** (bunking off) because he didn't want to see the **nitty nora** (school nurse). But he was **made up** (very pleased) to discover his teacher got **kaylied** (drunk) the night before and gave the **bootle buck** (battleaxe) a **kirby kiss** (head-butt) near the **lanny** (landing stage or pierhead).

SIMON ELMES

catercousin

close friend (Devon)

The Latin word *quattuor* means 'four', as in a rectangle with its four corners, and it is this that is at the heart of many words that include the dialect version of the Latin, **cater**, and that usually have the sense of something off at an angle or out of line. **Cater-cornered** means 'placed diagonally', to **cater-snozzle** is 'to make an angle', **cater-de-flamp** means 'all askew', **cater-slant** is 'out of shape', while **caterswish**, **-witch** and **-ways** all mean 'from side to side', such as when weaving drunkenly down a road.

It is from these wonderful beginnings that Devon's **catercousin** is likely to have developed, denoting one who is a friend, but not exactly a relation.

See also BLOOD, BREDREN, BUTTY, CHUCK, CLICK, CREW, HOMIE, MARRA, MUCKER, SORRY

champ

to mash; to crush (Scotland)

Champ, which is still alive and kicking, is also heard as **chamble** and is probably closely connected with **jam** and **jamble**, both of which mean to crush or squeeze violently. Hence **champing** can be the noisy grinding of teeth.

chamrag

to gossip (Wiltshire)

Cham, from champ, is another term for chew that is still to be found in Oxfordshire and the Isle of Wight, while **rag**, which may well have links to various Scandinavian terms meaning 'shagginess' or 'a strip of fur', was once a word for the tongue. Thus **chamrag**, a synonym for chatter, and indeed a literal equivalent to slang's 'chew the rag'.

See ALL THE LOCAL GOSSIP, p. 34, *and also* CANK, CANT, CLISH-MA-CLAVER, COOSE, JAFFOCK, JANGLE, NEIGHBOUR, PROSS, TALE-PYET

charver

a young person in trendy clothes and flashy jewellery (Cumbria, Liverpool and throughout the North-East)

Charvers are the **chavs** of the North-East. Charver (sometimes **charva**), was once used in Cumbria and Liverpool as a simple and affectionate term for a child, probably drawing on a Romany word *chavi* meaning just that. In the mid-1990s, however, it emerged in the North-East of Britain, from Middlesborough to the Scottish border at Berwick, as a term for a young working-class person, especially a woman, who wears cheap imitations of designer clothes and jewellery and who behaves in a loud, brash or loutish manner. Female charvers are often alternatively known as charvas or **kappa slappers**, which originated in Newcastle. Their male counterparts are known as **neds**, a modern sociological label similar to chavs. The characters Sandra and Tracy, the 'Fat Slags' in *Viz* magazine, are caricatures of charvers.

This sense of the word may (although this is as yet unproven) come from another Romany term *charver*, which means 'to have sex with': charver and kappa slapper both have clear sexual connotations, and indeed charver has also been used to refer specifically to a prostitute.

The following quote from the *Guardian* captures the prevailing image of the charver/charva: 'After dark, you can get twenty or so charvas loitering in the city's subway, drinking bottles of cider and shouting abuse at anyone who dares to challenge their territory, while spraying "Sarah is a slag" on the wall.'

See THE CHAVS AND THE CHAV-NOTS, p. 43, *and also* CHAV, JANNER, KAPPA SLAPPER, NED, PIKEY, SCALLY, TROBO

chav

a young person in trendy clothes and flashy jewellery (UK-wide, originally the South-East)

Chav may be the most controversial word in Britain of the past decade. The word was the first to reach national prominence from a whole list coined to describe the cultural phenomenon of young working-class people dressing in designer sportswear and flashy jewellery. It became shorthand for the phenomenon as a whole, and the focus of a considerable amount of state-of-the-nation chatter. What few realised when it exploded onto the scene in 2004 was that, far from being coined for our age, it had been around for over 150 years. It derives either from a Romany word meaning 'child', or a different Romany word meaning 'young male'. That means that, linguistically speaking, chavs can trace their origins back to ancient Sanskrit.

It is often said that chav is a contraction of Chatham, the place where 'chav culture' first began. The *Oxford English Dictionary* describes this theory as 'probably a later rationalization', but the common use of **townie** as a synonym in various parts of the country, and parallel words like **janner** and **trobo**, suggest that the name of Chatham may well have been an important secondary influence on the choice of the term chav.

Whatever its precise origin, it is likely that the history of chav is closely linked to **charver**, another word which has the same dual applications, one benign, the other derogatory.

See THE CHAVS AND THE CHAV-NOTS, p. 43, *and also* CHARVER, JANNER, KAPPA SLAPPER, NED, PIKEY, SCALLY, TROBO

The chavs and the chav-nots

'City centres aren't safe any more. It's because of the . . .' One of the hottest linguistic debates of recent years is whether the words that typically complete a sentence like that are inherently class-prejudiced. That's a difficult question, but what is undeniable about these words, which denote young people wearing designer sportswear and ostentatious jewellery, is that they generally follow a pattern where the lack of a standard word for an observable cultural phenomenon causes a proliferation of 'bottom up' terms for it, which in turn gives rise to regional variety. Both **chav** and **charver** are first recorded in local Internet newsgroups, while the earlier **ned** crops up in a dialect story. They are joined by the **bazza** or **fly boy** (North-East), a **gudgeon** (presumably another instance of using fish to mean 'stupid' or 'gullible'), a **hood** (Northern Ireland), a **nob**, **ratboy**, **skanger**, **steek**, **stig** or **townie** (Lancashire and further afield), and the **trev** and **yarco** (Great Yarmouth).

See also CHARVER, CHAV, JANNER, KAPPA SLAPPER, NED, PIKEY, SCALLY, TROBO

chiel
child (Scotland, north of England and the South-West)

Recorded in Scotland from the sixteenth century, and subsequently in Cumbria and Northumberland, **chiel** is really nothing more than a regional pronunciation of 'child'. This straightforward origin probably accounts for its usage much further south, namely in Dorset, Devon and Cornwall (*see* **babby**). In Thomas Hardy's *Far from the Madding Crowd*, it is said of the young Bathsheba Everdene that she 'was not at all a pretty chiel at that time'.

See SMALL TALK, p. 228, *and also* BABBY, BAIRN, WEAN

chin-cough

whooping cough (the Midlands, especially Birmingham)

In *Proper Brummie*, their fascinating collection of Birmingham words and phrases, Carl Chinn and Steve Thorne relate that, according to an ancient Midlands superstition, **chin-cough** can be cured if the afflicted child is taken out before sunrise on three consecutive mornings, and passed under and over a briar bush nine times. There were more worrying cures proposed elsewhere, including, in Warwickshire, the swallowing of a roasted mouse and, in Birmingham, taking children to gas-works to breathe in the air.

chuck, chuckie

friend (northern England and Scotland)

Chuck and the term of endearment **chuckie** are likely to be corruptions of 'chicken'. Shakespeare was one of the first users of chuck in *Love's Labour's Lost* ('the King would have me present the princess, sweet chuck, with some delightful ostentation').

See also BLOOD, BREDREN, BUTTY, CATERCOUSIN, CLICK, CREW, HOMIE, MARRA, MUCKER, SORRY

chuffed

pleased; satisfied (the North and Midlands)

Chuffed is generally defined as meaning happy. It has long been common in Yorkshire and Herefordshire, but it is now popular everywhere and has been since its first appearance in the middle of the twentieth century when it probably originated in the military. It is the ghost or relic of **chuff**, a seventeenth-century adjective in the North and Midlands meaning 'swollen' or 'chubby' – originally with literal fat but eventually with emotion. This in turn goes back to the largely obsolete sixteenth-century term chuff, which still survives in Cornwall. A chuff was 'a cheek swollen or puffed with fat and, by extension, the muzzle of beasts' (according to the *Oxford English*

Dictionary) but for that, sadly, no origin seems to have been discovered.

One Yorkshire glossary of 1876 even gives a couple of meaningless similes whose very existence proves that the word was extremely common, because it clearly assumed the meaning would be understood in spite of their unhelpfulness: 'as chuff as cheese' and 'as chuff as an apple' (perhaps these expressions were used to mean 'swollen with pride or conceited').

chuggypig
woodlouse (north Devon)

The **chuggypig**, and its companion the **nisseldraft**, are both fine examples of the ability of dialect to come up with charming names for what some might feel were less than wholly appealing creatures. Both terms denote a woodlouse, while the former has also been the runt of a litter of pigs as well as being used sometimes as a teasing term of affection. As one Devonian blogger put it recently, 'I baint laughed so much in yers, watch out for thuk chuggypig yer gert mump-aid.'

The humble woodlouse seems to inspire a number of names, including **cheesy bob** and, in the US, the **pill bug**. As regards its origins, chuggypig is linked to **chug**, 'to tug as a suckling child at the breast' (which may in turn link to slang's **chug-a-lug** and to **chug down** meaning to gulp down a drink). The nisseldraft's roots are more challenging, but probably tie into our standard terms nestle or nestling. Certainly the image of the woodlouse as a suckling babe is consistent – perhaps not an image for the squeamish.

clammed
hungry (Midlands, south Lancashire and south Yorkshire)

Clammed is probably an extended use of **clam**, a dialect variant of **clamp** with senses such as 'pinch', 'press', 'seize with force'. At the beginning of the twentieth century, it was recorded almost throughout England, but is now centred on the Midlands, especially the East.

See LEERY FOR LUNCH?, p. 106, *and also* CLEMT, HUNGERED, LEER/LEERY, YAP

clanger

a meat pasty (Lincolnshire)

> *See* HOGGAN

clart

mud (Scotland and the North-East)

> According to the *Oxford English Dictionary*, **clart** – which means 'sticky or claggy dirt' – is a very old word. It can be found, at least as **beclart**, 'covered in muck', as early as the thirteenth century. Thereafter it seems to have flown beneath the radar until the early nineteenth century when it re-emerged in Scotland as a term which extends beyond the muck itself to mean 'a dirty person', or 'a cheap and nasty thing'. It has subsequently spread as far south as the North-East, where it has the added development of hypocritical talk or flattery.
>
> *See* MUD, MUD, GLORIOUS MUD, p. 196, *and also* PLODGE, SLOB, SLUB, SLUCH

clemt

hungry (Lancashire)

> **Clemt** is a phonetic variation of **clemmed**, which in turn replicates **clammed**, a word that goes back to 'clam' and alludes to that particular bivalve's squeezing properties. It is a popular dialect term, with multiple meanings: 'to choke or be parched with thirst', 'to benumb with cold' and – as the noun **clem** – slow starvation. The **clemming house**, meanwhile, is where the butcher puts animals to starve prior to killing them. The wonderfully pithy **clemgut** or **clem vengeance**, meanwhile (reminiscent of slang's **belly-vengeance** for sour beer), is second-rate food. Finally (although the compounds go on and on), to be **clem-gutted** is to be ravenous.
>
> *See* LEERY FOR LUNCH?, p. 106, *and also* CLAMMED, HUNGERED, LEER/LEERY, THIRL, YAP

click

gang of friends (UK-wide but particularly London)

> **Click**, like **clique**, is thought to come from a clicking sound, and so
> the noise made by a group of people. Although very much a part of
> rap lyrics of the past decade or so, click amazingly goes back to the
> early nineteenth century. The *OED*'s first record of it is from 1822 with
> the sense of a narrow coterie or circle; a century later J. B. Priestley
> was writing, 'Local fellers, they was, all in a click, y'know, a gang.'

> *See also* BLOOD, BREDREN, BUTTY, CATERCOUSIN, CHUCK, CREW, HOMIE,
> MARRA, MUCKER, SORRY

clish-ma-claver

gossip (Scotland and Ulster)

> This Scots and Ulster word for gossip is a bit of a tautology: it is
> based on **clish** or **cleesh**, meaning to repeat an idle story, plus
> **claver**, which itself means an idle or pointless story or a piece of
> gossip. The duplication hardly matters though, such is the
> alliterative power of the term.

> *See* ALL THE LOCAL GOSSIP, p. 34, *and also* CANK, CANT, CHAMRAG, COOSE,
> JAFFOCK, JANGLE, NEIGHBOUR, PROSS, TALE-PYET

clocking

a snack, usually taken mid-morning (Staffordshire, Derbyshire,
Nottinghamshire and Warwickshire)

> Specifically referring to a mid-morning break, **clocking** was once
> more or less the equivalent of elevenses; the related **clocks** is
> found in Yorkshire. Nineteenth-century evidence shows that this
> snack break was often specifically associated with artisans in urban
> workshops and not just with rural labourers. The spread of the
> evidence through five of the core counties of the Industrial
> Revolution fits with this, and suggests that the word's popularity
> was the result of the new culture of working to the clock.

> *See* CLOCKING UP YOUR CROUSTS, p. 214, *and also* BAIT, JACKBIT, NUMMIT, SNAP,
> TOMMY

Clootie

the Devil (Scotland and northern England)

A cloot, in Scotland, is a division in the hoof of an ox or sheep, hence the name **Clootie** for the Devil, who is popularly represented with a cloven foot. Dialect is full of local epithets for the Devil, including **Auld Hornie** and **Dicky Devlin** (Yorkshire) and **Old Nick** in the South-East and elsewhere; Nick may be a shortened form of 'iniquity', another term for 'vice' in early modern English morality plays.

See also BEAT THE DEVIL ROUND THE GOOSEBERRY BUSH

clouts

clothes (northern England and Scotland)

The word **clout** was used in Anglo-Saxon English to refer to cloth and, in the plural, to swaddling clothes. From the thirteenth century on the plural form was commonly and contemptuously used to refer to clothes in general: such use has close analogies with **rags** and **weeds**, both of which were used in the same way from a slightly later date.

The proverb 'ne'er cast a clout till May be out' first appeared in the sixteenth century, while the proverbial simile 'as white (or pale) as a clout' can be found in the works of William Caxton, Shakespeare and Bunyan – in fact it can still be found in northern England.

Our daily bread

As befits such an essential source of food, there is in most languages a range of words for bread, which attest to regional diversity, variety and speciality, and which give credence to the idea that while the best wine may come from France, and the best tomatoes from Italy, the best bread always comes from home. In France, what qualifies as a *baguette* in Paris is different from the one you'll get in Lyon. Many British regions have distinctive styles that are part of the local identity, such as **soda bread** and the potato-based **boxty** in Ireland, and the fruity **bara brith** in Wales. Sadly for bread-lovers, we have spent most of the past century or so losing some prized local varieties, so that the East Anglian **dannock** (cooked in a frying pan) or the Scottish **mashloch** (a coarse multigrain bread) are now rarely or never seen. Fortunately for word-lovers, however, one type of basic bread has been and remains a focus of all sorts of local names – the humble bread roll.

Roll in this sense was first used in the latter part of the sixteenth century, but quickly established itself as the standard term. As the English of south-eastern England became the basis for standard educated English over the course of the eighteenth century, so a large number of dialect alternatives arose, particularly in the North and the Midlands. These ranged from the very general, like **bap** and **cob**, which typically have now spread, at least to some extent, southwards, to the more distinctively local, such as the **stotty** of the North-East or the **tommy** of the South-West. At the extreme, **batch** seems largely restricted to the area around Coventry. What is sure is that anyone from the North or Midlands, visiting the South and using the word they grew up with to ask in a shop for a cheese roll, runs the risk of receiving not their lunch, but a quizzical, slightly suspicious look.

See also BAP, BARM CAKE, BUTTY, COB, MANSHON, NUBBIES, STOTTY

cob

bread roll (northern England)

For a three-letter monosyllable, **cob** is a remarkably industrious little word. The basic images are those of size and stoutness (a stack of corn, a small island, a hard mass), of something that is rounded or humped (a nut, a kernel, a baked apple-dumpling) and something that, like the head, stands on top (a leader, a tuft of hair on the forehead). It is, however, probably as bread that it is best known, a sense that falls into the 'rounded or humped' category, giving the cob or cob-loaf, which is essentially a small loaf of bread or a small cake made of the very last piece of dough from a baking. It can also be a kind of muffin.

There are cobs in Shakespeare, or to be more precise, there is a reference in *Troilus and Cressida* to a **coblofe** (i.e. cob-loaf). This just means 'round loaf' or 'lump-shaped loaf', and is one of a number of uses of the word to refer to a roundish mass or object, such as a nut or a small haystack, but by the nineteenth century, the cob had, in terms of bread, come to mean specifically 'a small round bread roll'. It was used chiefly in the north of England, and although it has, like **bap**, spread more widely in recent years, it is still more common in the North and Midlands. Another meaning of cob, common in northern England in the nineteenth century, was 'testicle'; luckily though, there are no accounts of unfortunate misunderstandings.

See OUR DAILY BREAD, p. 49, *and also* BAP, BARMCAKE, BUTTY, MANSHON, NUBBIES, STOTTY

(have a) cob on

a bad mood, a sulk (chiefly Liverpool and Midlands)

You can **have a cob on**, or **get a cob on**. The phrase originated in
the Merchant Navy and then passed into the language of Britain's
greatest merchant port, Liverpool, from where it eventually spread
across the North Midlands. It has been suggested that it is linked to
the widespread dialect sense of **cob**, 'a blow to the head', but this is
only speculation. It's also common to get a **bag on** or a **nark on** in
the same region.

See THE MARDY BLUES, p. 134, *and also* MARDY, TATCHY

cobnut

a children's game similar to conkers (the South-West but also in
pockets across the UK)

Cobnut, **cobblety-nut** or **cob-joe** are all names for a children's
game which, in extracting the cobnut's kernel, putting it on a string
and challenging your fellow nut-brandishers to a battle, seems to
have been a parallel or perhaps earlier form of conkers. As
recorded in *Notes and Queries* (a 'medium of inter-
communication' for 'readers and writers, collectors and librarians',
published in England since the mid-nineteenth century) in 1890:
'There were many formulas and observances in the game of
"cobnut" . . . If a couple of wax ends become twizzled, the boy
who first could shout, "Twizzler, twizzler! my fost blow," took the
first stroke . . . When a nut was cracked so that a piece came out,
the owner . . . called out, "Jick, jack, gell, ar shonner pley thy shell,"
he took the damaged nut . . . On the contrary, if the owner of the
damaged nut could first call out, "Jick, jack, gell, an you sholl pley
my shell," both were bound to go on till the one or other was
completely smashed.'

A conker, incidentally, took its name from a term popular in East
Anglia and Shropshire for a snail-shell – which in turn probably took
its name from the standard word conqueror.

cock-a-hoop

happy (UK-wide but originally in Merseyside)

The phrase **cock-a-hoop** originates from the early sixteenth century, when it was also known as 'setting the cock on the hoop'. There are many theories as to the story behind it. A seventeenth-century glossary notes that 'our Ancestors call'd that the Cock which we call a Spigget . . . the Cock being taken out, and laid on the hoop of the vessel, they used to drink up the ale as it ran out without intermission . . . then they were Cock-on-Hoop, i.e. at the height of mirth and jollity.'

The story is a nice one, but there is no clear evidence of the use of the word cock for spigot, and the matter is further complicated by the use of figures in tavern-signs from a much earlier date, some of which still exist. Nonetheless, there was certainly a historical connection between being cock-a-hoop and supremely drunk. Today, though, the term means simply to be 'elated and exultant', or 'loudly triumphant', whether or not alcohol has been involved.

combe-downer

a short measure of beer (Bath)

If you are given a **combe-downer**, you will feel short-changed, for it is a beer glass which isn't quite as full as it should be. The history of the term is a lovely and very local one: it is said that the stonemasons working down at the limestone mines at Combe Down near Bath in the eighteenth and nineteenth centuries would ask their young apprentices to go and fetch them some beer from the local inn. The boys, in a hurry over the rough terrain of the quarries, would inevitably spill some of the ale they were so diligently carrying. The result? The chastising words 'That's a bit of a Combe-Downer', a lament (albeit a more affectionate one) you can still hear in pockets of Somerset to this day when a poured refreshment isn't quite what it ought to be.

coopy down

to squat (the South-West and particularly Bristol)

To **coopy down** is to crouch down or to squat, and offers the image of fitting one's body into a coop, or narrow, confined space. A **coopy** house is a very small house or other kind of building, and reflects standard English's cubby-hole, which has been linked to a variety of Teutonic words meaning a 'lean-to for cattle' or the Dutch *kub*, a form of basket for fish.

coose

to gossip (Cornwall and the West Country)

Meaning to gossip or chat, **coose** goes back to Old Cornish **cows**, and that in turn to French *causer*, both of which meant 'to gossip'. This seems to be linked to French *chose*, 'a thing' (about which one is chatting or gossiping), and beyond that to Latin's *causari*, 'to plead or dispute, to argue, or to make objections for the purpose of gaining time'. Quite a long history for such an earthy-sounding word.

See ALL THE LOCAL GOSSIP, p. 34, *and also* CANK, CHAMRAG, CLISH-MA-CLAVER, JAFFOCK, JANGLE, NEIGHBOUR, PROSS, TALE-PYET

crabbit

bad-tempered (Scotland)

Crabbit is no more than the Scottish pronunciation of **crabbed**, and it too means 'grumpy' or 'ill-tempered'. Its immediate image is that of the crab apple – and in this case its sourness. Curiously, the name of the apple itself derives from a different meaning of crabbed, one which the *OED* describes as 'the crooked or wayward gait of the crustacean, and the contradictory, perverse, and fractious disposition which this expressed'. When extended to the world of fruit, the image is that of a gnarled, unappetising apple. As for people with the tendency to be crabbit, they are, 'sour-tempered, morose, peevish and harsh'.

craic

fun, enjoyment (Ireland)

The Irish word **craic**, which has endured for centuries as the pithiest of expressions for a good time (and a whole lot more besides), enjoyed a vast surge in mass consciousness with the burgeoning of Irish theme pubs across the UK and the US, the doors of which promised, amid many other emerald green stereotypes, 'good craic'. The term means 'good fellowship', with plenty of (often well-lubricated) merry chat. It is quite simply a wonderful part of the Irish lexicon, and one that is rooted in a fourteenth-century meaning of the verb **crack** of saying something with a sense of abruptness or éclat. It is a linguistic partner with the word crack meaning a joke, and indeed with the Scottish and northern English **cracking on** in the sense of chattering.

crew

gang of friends (UK-wide but particularly major cities)

Crew goes back at least as far as the sixteenth century, when it was a synonym for the wandering bands of criminal beggars. In 1970s America, the word became a by-word in the hip-hop subculture for a group of rappers, breakdancers, graffiti artists, etc. who were working or performing together. It then later became extended to a person's friends, associates or entourage. Like **click**, and so much else in modern slang, the word was reborn in black English before moving out into the mainstream.

See also BLOOD, BREDREN, BUTTY, CATERCOUSIN, CHUCK, CLICK, HOMIE, MARRA, MUCKER, SORRY

croggy

a stolen apple; a pillion ride on a bicycle (the North-East; Cornwall and Devon; Leicestershire, Nottinghamshire and Teesside)

For those living in Teesside, a **croggy** is a stolen apple, scrumped, as generations of the young have put it, from someone else's apple tree. And, so they say, the word comes from **oggie raidin**, i.e. orchard raiding. That said, if you move down to Leicestershire, a croggy can be a ride hitched on a friend's bicycle. Further south still and you can find the dish, from the South-West, known as **tiddy oggy**, which brings us back to the apple (along with pork, Dijon mustard and a few other things). And there is yet one more meaning too: the *English Dialect Dictionary* defines croggy as 'weak in the foreleg' (of a horse).

None of which wholly helps us as to the linguistic origin of the word. The best guess is that the northern and West-Country **oggy** is at the root of it (and that perhaps we steal or cadge, as it were, the ride on the crossbar). But other theories suggest a link to *crog*, which is Gaelic for 'paw', and so the hand that steals the apple. There is finally one other possibility: Cornwall's home-grown **croggan**, a limpet shell, an image that makes sense if you think of the two riders, one clinging tightly to the other.

See also HOGGAN, OGGY

croosle

to whine; to whimper (Devon)

Croosle has a variety of meanings, including 'whimpering like an infant just waking up', 'gossiping, flattering, courting favour' or 'talking confidentially'. Given that the *English Dialect Dictionary* stresses that 'a fretful or peevish tone is always implied' it is possible that there is some link to being **cross**. Its slightly different spelling, **creusle**, is also Devonian, and means 'to grumble', 'to complain' or, with infants still in mind, 'to grizzle'.

cuddy-wifter

a left-handed person (Scotland and northern England)

The adjective **cuddy-handed** has long meant left-handed in England's North, and the curious term **cuddy-wifter** is quite simply a left-handed person. First, the easy one: **wifter** is synonymous with **waft**, a gesture that's seen to brush the air away, and itself a development from **whiff**, a puff of air.

Cuddy, however, is less straightforward. We do know that it has been a Scottish term for a donkey since at least the early eighteenth century; it has, as the *Oxford English Dictionary* suggests, the same 'homely status' for the Scots as donkey does for the English. One theory suggests that cuddy is a diminutive form of the proper name Cuthbert, and so echoes such other donkey nicknames as Neddy and Dicky. Another suggestion, from Jamieson in his major Scottish dictionary of 1808, is that there is a Romany root. Unfortunately it would appear that no such name exists in any of the Gypsy dialects (the Scottish Gypsy term for a donkey, for instance, was **eizel**, which comes from German). So quite what the linguistic path to cuddy-handed and cuddy-wifter is remains unclear. One possibility is, if we understand the southpaw (as left-handers are called in boxing circles) to be considered as a figurative ass – i.e. clumsy, a cuddy-wifter would then be a donkey (-like) waver of the hands. Left-handers have never had an easy ride (but then neither have donkeys).

See also KAY-LEGGED, KEER-HANDED

culchie

a provincial, a rustic (Ireland)

> **Culchie** is Belfast's word of choice to deride a peasant or a country bumpkin. It was coined at University College, Galway to describe the agricultural students there. Today it is largely used in Dublin of someone from any other part of Ireland.
>
> It has a variety of roots, all based on the town of Coillte Mach (i.e. Kiltimagh) in County Mayo. Brendan Behan in his *Confessions of an Irish Rebel* (1965) recalls how, 'One night, Culchiemachs, as we call the Irish-speaking people, wished to play a game of pitch and toss.' The word **coillte** itself means 'woods', and finally the **cúl a' tí** was the back door of a great house, to which peasants would, apparently, be directed.

cushty

fine; dandy (London and UK-wide)

> The golden age of the catchphrase may have waned in recent times, but TV, even in today's all-cable, all channel-surfing wonderland, has its part to play. While *Minder*, the series about the London underworld that ran from 1979 to 1994, gave us **'er indoors**, not long afterwards *Only Fools and Horses* added **cushty**, meaning 'wonderful, first-rate' or 'magic', to the popular lexicon. The word, which is linked to the more widely used **cushy**, comes from Romany *kushto*, *kushti*, 'good' (used unvarnished by nineteenth-century market traders), and ultimately, thanks to Romany origins in India, from Hindi *khush*, 'pleasure'.

dab hand

an expert, a practised doer of something (originally the East End of London, now UK-wide)

In this well-known phrase, the **hand** means a person, using the process known as metonymy – whereby the specific object is used to denote the greater whole – to do so. Meanwhile **dab** is an old word, beginning life in late seventeenth-century criminal slang, where it means one who is 'expert, exquisite in Roguery' (as the *Oxford English Dictionary* has it). From there it passed on to gambling jargon, where it described a top-flight gamester, and around 1900 seemed especially popular among schoolboys who could be **dabs** at cricket or classics. Those who read translations of the work of social chronicler Honoré de Balzac will be familar with the use of dab to describe his master-criminal Vautrin (himself based on a real-life master-thief-turned-thief-taker Vidocq, who later became Paris's chief of police). Its origins remain obscure, although it has been tied to Latin *dabo*, 'I give' – presumably, in this case, referring to expertise.

daft

silly (chiefly the North)

> **Daft** has been used since Anglo-Saxon times. Originally it meant 'mild, gentle', but it went on to develop the sense 'silly' by the fourteenth century at the latest. It has always been a predominantly northern and Scottish word. Although now known throughout England (if a little less common in the South-East), it remains characteristically northern, so that the song 'Everyone Thinks He Looks Daft', by the Leeds band The Wedding Present, can be seen as implicitly asserting a real northern identity.

> *See* DON'T BE DAFT, p. 89, *and also* ADDLE-HEADED, BARMY, FOND, GORM-LESS, QUILT, SOFT

daggy

old-fashioned (UK-wide but particularly the North-East)

> A **dag** is a clotted lump of wool and dung that hangs from the fleece surrounding a sheep's rear end. They cannot of course be alone in such accessories, but the sheep tend to be Australians or New Zealanders – at least that's where the word originates. So too does the adjective **daggy**, meaning 'tedious', 'conservative' and 'socially unacceptable' not to mention 'scruffy' and 'unclean'. In this case it appears to have quit the Antipodes to tour its European home. Or at least Britain's school playgrounds where it remains a popular term of abuse.

daps

soft shoes (Wales and Wiltshire)

> **Daps** originally referred to slippers, but today are what have been termed plimsolls, gym shoes and currently trainers, even if the simple dap is unlikely to offer the kind of bells and whistles the modern wearer forks out so much to display. The term is possibly linked to their slapping along the ground: there is a verb 'to dap',

again that little bit onomatopœic, which refers to the bounce of a ball – and so the image might well be of bouncing along in your rubber-soled shoes. One other theory is that the term developed from an earlier verb meaning 'to hop and skip'. It seems to have been local to the South-West and South Wales ever since its first appearance in the 1920s, and it remains the standard word in that area. Dylan Thomas refers to a pair of lost daps in his story 'The Map of Love.'

See ANYONE FOR SANNIES? p. 99, *and also* GUTTIES, PUMPS, SANNIES

dardledumdue

daydreamer (East Anglia)

Dardledumdue is a beautiful old East Anglian word for a daydreamer. Unfortunately the story ends there, for there seems to be no clue available as to where it comes from. The term conjures up an image of some happy peasant, straw drooping from his lips, a donkey's battered straw hat borrowed to keep off the bees, ambling along some country lane singing some tuneless 'dumdeedumdee' tune. But any interpretation has to be subjective, and perhaps it is part of the beauty of the word that dardledumdue can mean whatever we want it to.

daunder

to saunter; to idle (Scotland and northern England)

Daunder is a variation on the more widely used **dander**. Not the dander you can get up, but the one that means 'to saunter, stroll or wander', as well as 'to waste time' and even 'to hobble'. Hence comes **danderer**, a wanderer or time-waster, and the **dandering-Kate**, a plant more formally known as the stone orpine or stonecrop (and which is also known as the livelong). Daunder joins other onomatopœic words denoting similar activities, or lack of them, including **mooching**, **pootling** and **footling**.

No mean feet

Words for **splay-footed** bear many resemblances, unsurprisingly, to those for pigeon-toed. Splay-footed is, like pigeon-toed, an uncomplicated descriptive term, but it is considerably older (mid-sixteenth century) and has an established history of use in standard, literary sources from the beginning. If it stayed constant for centuries, however, its counterparts in dialect make up a dazzlingly long list – one, in fact, of the longest of any subject. Here are just some of them:

bat-footed (Essex, Suffolk), **bedlam-feet**, **broad-arrowed** (Somerset), **broad-footed**, **broad-toed**, **cow-heeled**, **dew-footed** (Norfolk), **duck-footed** (North), **ducky-feet**, **four o'clock** (Berkshire), **goose-footed** (Durham), **lady forward** (North Wales), **open-toed**, **pin-toed**, **plaw-footed**, **pratt-footed** (Kent), **pumple-footed** (Somerset), **quarter-past-nine** (Somerset), **quarter-to-five** (Wiltshire), **quarter-to-four** (Norfolk), **quarter-to-nine** (Lancashire, Cornwall), **quarter-to-three** or **quarter-to-two** (the South-West), **rab-footed**, **scrabble-footed** (Somerset), **scrog-footed**, **scrush-footed**, **shovel-footed** (Nottinghamshire, Lancashire), **scrog-footed** (Suffolk), **skew-footed**, **slab-footed**, **sly-footed** (Isle of Man), **splar-foot**, **splar-footed**, and **splatter-foot**,

deegle

a stolen marble (Cheshire)

> In his lively compendium of extraordinary words *The Meaning of Whiffling*, Adam Jacot de Boinod lists just a few of the many names for marbles in the north-east of England. They include **alleys**, **boodies**, **glassies**, **liggies**, **marvels**, **muggles**, **penkers**, **parpers**, and **scudders**. In addition to these nicknames, there is a local lexicon for marble-playing that survives to this day. To **deegle** is, in Cheshire, to pilfer or steal, while in the same county a **cheeny** or a **crodle** is a large marble, and a **Spotted Dick** a flecked one. A **neggy-lag**, in Yorkshire, is the penultimate shot in a game of marbles, while **flirt** takes on a whole new meaning in Yorkshire where it means 'to flick a marble with your finger and thumb'.

splatter-footed, **splawdered**, **splawder-foot**, **splawder-footed**, **splawdy-footed** (Yorkshire, Lincolnshire), **sprawled** (West Glamorgan), **sprawl-footed** (East Wales), **sprog-hocked** (Staffordshire), **ten-to-two**, **Wednesday-and-Thursday** (Norfolk), **wem-footed** (Norfolk), **wide-feet** (Berkshire), **wide-foot** (Kent) and **wide-footed** (Devon, Norfolk).

Some of these are undeniably evocative. In Norfolk, **Wednesday-and-Thursday** suggests your feet don't even know what day of the week it is. The Kentish **pratt-footed** seems to mean 'buttock-footed', although it is unclear whether this is just descriptive or involves implicit criticism or contempt. The latter can be seen in the Manx **sly-footed** and perhaps in **lady forward** from North Wales. Even the purely descriptive variants are frequently more vividly creative than their pigeon-toed equivalents, like **broad-arrowed** or **sprog-hocked** (which derives from a dialect word meaning 'a fork in a tree branch'). Possibly the most common type of formation now involves envisaging the person's feet as the hands of a clock telling the time as **ten-to-two**, **quarter-to-three**, or (in Wiltshire, where some people must have double-jointed ankles) **quarter-to-five**.

See also DEW-FOOTED, PASTY-FOOTED

dew-footed

splay-footed (Norfolk)

The dew in **dew-footed** is used here in its completely standard meaning. So how on earth can feet pointing slightly apart be like the dew? The answer appears if you discover that Norfolk dialect also contains two nouns denoting someone who is splay-footed: **dew-dasher** and **dew-sweeper**. And so the image is in fact rather poetic, for dew-footed could be defined as 'sweeping up the dew with one's feet'.

See NO MEAN FEET, above, *and also* PASTY-FOOTED

dimpsy

sleepy; dusky (Devon)

The use of the word **dimpsy** to mean 'sleepy' suggests an intriguing link between two ideas with which it is connected: twilight and haziness.

In Devon, you might hear that 'it's getting a bit dimpsy'; in other words, dusk is falling. The adjective dimpsy comes from the word **dimps**, meaning twilight, and which may be derived from dim, in this case referring to fading light.

Dimps may, however, also be a variant of the word **dumps**, which has had various meanings over time, among them 'a dazed or puzzled state of mind', or 'a fit of melancholy' (in the dumps). Dumps itself probably comes from a Low German/Dutch word meaning 'haze' or 'mist' – again suggestive perhaps of a sleepy state.

See also DUMMETS

dirt deen

tired out, exhausted (north-east Scotland)

Recorded principally in Aberdeen since the beginning of the twentieth century, **dirt** is an adverbial use of a noun employed as a contemptuous or offensive epithet (as in 'He's a dirt'). **Deen** is the past participle of **dae**, the Scottish form of do, so the whole means 'done to dirt' (or something ruder).

See ALL PAGGERED AND POOTLED, p. 115, *and also* BLETHERED, BUSHWHA, JIGGERED, LAMPERED, MAGGLED, WABBIT

dobby

a household spirit said to haunt certain premises or localities (Sussex and the Lake District)

The word **dobbie** is probably an altered form of Robbie, the pet-name for Robin. This has been the source of many a name for imps and spirits, including **hobgoblin** (of which hob is another form), and

Robin Goodfellow – a mischievous elf who was said to haunt the English countryside in the sixteenth and seventeenth centuries. In Sussex, the sprite also goes by the name of **Master Dobbs**.

dog

a bottle of beer (Newcastle)

> **Dog** is a term that embraces a wide variety of meanings, especially in slang. As far as specifically local usages are concerned, the most recent is probably the one in Newcastle for a bottle of beer, the local **Newky Brown**. This sense of the term emerged during the 1980s when a new advertising campaign, entitled 'The Dog', exploited the local euphemism of 'I'm going to walk the dog', meaning 'I'm off to the pub for a bottle of Newcastle Brown Ale'. The ad featured a finger in the process of opening a can, giving the sound *Wooof!* as the air rushed out.

dog

to play truant (Cheshire)

> In the course of the local interviews undertaken for the BBC's Voices Project, the word **dog** emerged as a synonym in Cheshire for playing truant. Despite the lack of evidence for this sense of the word in both the *English Dialect Dictionary* and the *OED*, there is a large body of evidence in American printed records, from the 1920s onwards, for the phrase to **dog it**, meaning 'to shirk', 'to waste time', 'to malinger', or 'to act lazily'. This may well be one of thousands of terms that were part of the great movement of American slang across the Atlantic after the Second World War.

> *See* BUNKING AND PLUNKING, p. 192, *and also* BUNK OFF, MITCH, NICK OFF, PLAY HOOKEY PLUNK, SAG, SKIDGE, SKIVE, TWAG, WAG

How to talk like ... a Geordie

'Geordie' is how people often refer loosely to anyone from the north-east of England. Yet the term is strictly speaking applied only to denizens of the city of Newcastle and their accent: 'Morpethian's Morpethian,' says with pride an elderly inhabitant of the nearby market town of Morpeth, 'an' thah aul differen" – 'they're all different!' So I shall here speak more fittingly perhaps about a *Northumbrian* accent, with a particular Tyneside city variety that ranges from the fringe of Wearside to the south and just a little up the coast into the former mining area to the north.

The Northumbrian accent lies at the diametrical opposite end of the 'accent appreciation index' to the speech of those other two great English urban centres, Liverpool and Birmingham. Geordie almost always comes top in favourite accent surveys and it's said that call centres used to like to recruit staff from Northumberland because they naturally spoke in 'warm and friendly' tones. Now of course, an angry fight in Newcastle is no less ugly than one on Merseyside, but it's true that it's hard not to smile on leaving the train at Newcastle station, surrounded as the visitor is by the lilting 'song' of Geordie speech. Northumbrian has a rising inflection which combines with the many glottal stops (momentary slivers of silence, here breathed into something far more substantial than their Cockney cousin). So 'proper' becomes 'pro'ah' – 'pro'ah oould women' ('proper old women'); but it goes much further.

There's no rhoticity (r-sounding) in Geordie, so where in other parts of the country we'd readily insert a rogue 'r' to form expressions like the now familiar 'lauranorder' (law and order), in the North-East this just doesn't happen. Here they insert a little hiatus, a fractional stop, which combines very naturally with the modified vowel sounds of Geordie, and the ubiquitous 'ah' sound. 'Thah–'aul differen',' said our lady from Morpeth, where 'thah–' represents my attempt to render the Northumbrian version of 'they are' followed by one of those little characteristic hiccups which give the accent its delicious jerkiness.

So Geordie has a distinctive tune, a very recognisable rhythm; what about the notes themselves? Well, unsurprisingly, much of the heart of what makes Geordie *Geordie* lies in the vowels. And in pride of place comes the sound you hear day in, day out on Tyneside, which I'll render here as 'iuh', and it's the Northumbrian version of the sound in 'day in, day out' which in Byker becomes the diphthong 'diuh'. So if a gadgie (bloke) asks your 'niuhm' he's asking what you're called; and if he wants you not to hang about over it, he'll tell you to say it striUHT-aWIUH, or *straight away*.

In Northumbrian, also, the 'aye's have it – not only is it the normal word for 'yes', but the sound itself, with a strongly pronounced 'y' in it, crops up all over the place and is one of the accent's most obvious characteristics, so *nice* becomes 'niyce', *mile*, 'miyle', and that quintessential area of Newcastle, called Byker, is 'BIYY-kah'. In fact there's a tendency to insert this 'y' sound everywhere, so *married* becomes 'marriyd' and *again* is 'aGIYuhn'.

'Wor' is a sound that covers both *our* ('wor awn house' is *our own house*) and *were*, so 'We wor happy to have wor awn house' is the proud boast of the Tyneside home-owner, or 'hoouhm-oouhner' as a local would say it. Up here the open 'o' sound of *oats*, *home*, *open*, and that sad phenomenon of economic downturns not just in the North-East the *dole*, is another marked diphthong with a strong bend in the middle, 'oouhts', 'hoouhm', 'oouhpn' and 'doouhl'. Except of course in the word *nobody* which is, Scots-fashion, 'naebody', and in the tag expression *you know*, which is always 'yi nah'.

Finally on these rich Newky vowels, I must mention the way the long vowels 'er' and 'or' sound. So words like *work*, *furniture* and *first* all now seem to have 'aw' in the middle – 'wawk', 'fawniture' and 'fawst', and conversely *all* becomes 'ahl'. To the standard northern 'oo' for 'u' (*lucky* is 'looky') you can add those juicy local formations like 'divvent' for *don't* and a host of classic dialectal terms – hinny, pet, canny and the rest – and you've brewed up a distinctive accent that's made its way firmly into the popular imagination through TV hits like *Auf Wiedersehen, Pet* and the County Durham-set film *Billy Elliot*.

So in the **pit raas** (pit rows) of north-east England, a **bairn** (child) can grow up to be not a chav as elsewhere in the country, but a **chava** or **charver**, the Geordie term for a young guy with attitude. He can find life **canny** (nice) or even **canny nice** (which is presumably twice as nice), or indeed **cushty** (excellent). He would never *go* anywhere but, as in the famous song 'Blaydon Races', **gan** ('ye should've seen us **gannin'**'). He would certainly **gan hyem** (go home) each night to see his **hinny**, after working with his **marras** (mates), unless he'd had a bad day and was feeling **radgy** (angry). In which case he might head down to the pub and sink a pint of local Radgie **Gadgie** (man) ale (brewed at the Mordue Brewery, Wallsend), though these days he'd have to stand outside to light up a **tab** (cigarette)!

SIMON ELMES

doolally

mad, crazy (London and now UK-wide)

Doolally, or in full **doolally tap**, is one of the linguistic survivors of the old British Raj, and of the Army that backed it up. The term came from the Deolali military sanatorium in Bombay, to which mentally ill troops were sent at the close of the nineteenth century. However, according to the veteran Frank Richards, writing in his memoir *Old Soldier Sahib* (1936), the illness came not before one arrived at Deolali but during one's stay there. Time-expired troops were sent to the sanatorium to await the next troop-ship home. It was during the long hot days of tedium that men, formerly first-class soldiers, might gradually go to pieces. Going doolally was their pronunciation of their fate at Deolali.

doup

backside (Scotland)

'I'll kick your doup!' is an expression many a Scottish child will have heard, and feared. **Doup** is pronounced 'dowp' and can mean the bottom end of anything, especially if it is round in shape. Its origin is unknown but it may derive from **dolp**, which is the bottom of an eggshell.

down the banks

getting annoyed with (Liverpool)

We can thank Liverpool's Irish community for the colourful expression **down the banks**, which apparently refers to nothing more sophisticated than peat bogs, down the steep banks of which unfortunate people might roll, ending up immersed in the deep, peaty water. P. W. Joyce's *English As We Speak It In Ireland* (1910) offers the alternative phrase to **give someone down the banks**, meaning 'to scold or reprimand'. Amazingly, exactly that same formulation can be found across the Atlantic 25 years earlier, namely in Mark Twain's *Huckleberry Finn* of 1884.

doxy

a sweetheart (UK-wide but particularly London and Cornwall)

In dialect use, the adjective **doxy** means 'dainty', 'petite', 'smart' or 'pretty'; as a noun it means 'a sweetheart' or 'a young girl'. But the same word can also be a negative, describing a slattern or overdressed old woman (often referring to a man's wife). In either context its definition is a mystery. It may be based on Dutch *docke*, meaning 'a doll', which of course means 'girl' in English slang as well, or, with the accent still on slang, there may be a punning link to **dock** meaning 'tail', and thus a 'piece of tail'. This would certainly work for doxy's earliest known use, in the criminal slang of the sixteenth century, where it describes the mistress of a rogue or beggar and, often synonymously, a promiscuous woman or even a prostitute. Here she might be an **arch-doxy**, in which case her 'boyfriend' was the gang's boss, or a **doxy-dell**, which is literally a doubling, 'promiscuous woman-promiscuous woman', and which, unsurprisingly, means 'a whore'.

dreckly

directly; in a while (Devon and Cornwall)

Dreckly is almost always part of the stereotypical Devonian phrase-book. And yet, unlike so many dialect impersonations, it is genuinely still used. Although a local pronunciation of directly, it is not quite that simple, for **dreckly** more often than not means 'when I get around to it', or even 'I'll do it later'. A little like the Spanish *mañana*, in fact.

drouthie

thirsty (Scotland)

Drought, the state of rainlessness, tends to be applied to countries and their landscapes, but the Scottish **drouthie**, which draws on the same word, means 'thirsty', and definitely applies to humans. Not only that, but it can also mean 'addicted to drink' (and not water either). Glasgow spells things a little differently – **droothy** – but the meanings are the same.

Liquid lunches

Anything can mean 'drunk' – especially if it is in the form 'I got -ed last night'. A nowhere-near-exhaustive list of current slang terms could include **muntered, mullered, pissed, blitzed, wrecked, trashed, plastered, sloshed, shit-faced, wasted, bombed, canned, loaded, buzzed, bevvied, hammered, wasted, tipsy, bladdered, rat-arsed, steaming, smashed, wankered, slaughtered, trolleyed, blottered, three sheets to the wind, merry, half-cut, tiddly, blathered, blotto, lashed** or **pie-eyed**. And that's just for starters.

Interestingly, most of these expressions are fairly recent, and they seem to have replaced a similar wealth of dialect terms from the nineteenth century. For example, someone could be **beerified, foxed, kaylied** or **faxt** in West Yorkshire, **rory** in Scotland or **corned** in the Midlands, or **corny** in the East (both apparently deriving from an old word describing beer with a strong malt taste). One could be **hoddy-doddy** in Devon (which means that a drunken Devonian visiting Lancashire and finding himself the butt of an **April Fool** would have been a hoddy-doddy niddy-noddy!). The principal dialect forms today are centred in Scotland and Ireland, which probably says less about the drinking per se in those countries than it does about the role of drink in their literary cultures and the brilliance of the writers who have written about it.

See also BLOOTERED, DRUCKEN, DRUFFEN, FLUTHERED, MALLETED, PISHED, PUGGLED, SKIMMISHED, STOCIOUS

drucken

drunk (Scotland and northern England)

> A northern variant of drunken, **drucken** is of Scandinavian origin. It was recorded in southern Scotland and in England north of Derbyshire by the *English Dialect Dictionary* (1902), but by the Survey of English Dialects, taken in the 1950s, it had become restricted to Yorkshire. It goes a long way back: it is recorded of a

young Lancastrian man of the nineteenth century that he 'gets blin' drucken amang his mates'.

See LIQUID LUNCHES, p. 70, *and also* BLOOTERED, DRUFFEN, FLUTHERED, MALLETED, PISHED, PUGGLED, SKIMMISHED, STOCIOUS

druffen
drunk (Yorkshire)

Druffen was common in West Yorkshire in the nineteenth century and was still recorded there by the Survey of English Dialects in the 1950s, which also discovered it just over the border in Lancashire. It is probably just an alteration of drunken.

See also LIQUID LUNCHES, p. 70, *and also* BLOOTERED, DRUCKEN, FLUTHERED, MALLETED, PISHED, PUGGLED, SKIMMISHED, STOCIOUS

duffy
ugly (Liverpool)

Duffy is a Caribbean word transplanted to Liverpool, which has one of the oldest West Indian communities in the country – hardly surprising when you think of Liverpool's history as Britain's major transatlantic port. Duffy seems to derive from the Caribbean word *duppy*. In Jamaican folklore, the *duppy* was a ghost or spirit of a dead person capable of returning to the earth to help or (usually) harm a living person. The same tradition is recorded in other parts of the Caribbean and in the American South. It is clearly of African origin, and the word derives from *dupe*, 'ghost', in the Bube language (one of the Bantu languages of West Africa). Duffy is used to describe a sexually unattractive person; the implication appears to be that to be approached by that person is as frightening as being set upon by a duppy.

See THE MIRROR CRACKED, p. 31, *and also* BUTTERS, FUSTY, LAIDLY, MINGING, MUNTER, OBZOCKY, RANK, SKANK

dummets

dusk (the South-West)

> **Dummets** is a pleasing word which, like Devon's **dimpsy**, suggests the softness of fading light: the dusk or twilight. And like the natural fading of the day its origins are simple: the standard English **dim**, which itself comes from Old English **dimm**, meaning 'obscure', or 'dark'. Simple it may be, but it is also very beautiful.

> *See also* DIMPSY

dunny

a lavatory or privy (Scotland and Australia)

> The **dunny** is the modern abbreviation of an old word from criminal slang – **dunekin** (or **dunegan**, **dunnakin**, **dunniken** and **dunyken**, with further variations **dunnigan** and **dunnee** in Australia). Dunekin itself was a combination of two cant or criminal slang words: **danna**, meaning human or other excrement (and itself perhaps from **dung**), and **ken**, meaning a place or house. Among less savoury nineteenth-century occupations was that of driving the **danna-drag** (drag meaning 'a horse-drawn vehicle') or nightsoil cart, emptying cesspits and privies while their daytime users slept. The **dunnigan** or **donegan worker** was, however, not the man who sat on the danna-drag. Instead he was a thief, at least in 1930s America, who hung round public lavatories, hoping to steal from discarded coats or to take parcels or any other items that had been foolishly left unattended.

emmet

ant; a tourist (Cornwall)

Emmet is rooted in the Old English word **aemette**, which, on the basis of either dropping or hanging onto the median vowel, can be found in two synonymous English words: ant, the standard, and emmet, the dialect version. Its first appearance is in a ninth-century Kentish glossary, where **emetan** is the word chosen to translate the Latin *formicae*. From this early start it has remained a dialect term. In the nineteenth century it meant a 'lively person', at least in Northants, but it is in its modern use, and in the holiday county of Cornwall, that it has gained its best-known definition.

An emmet today is likely to be the term of choice for one of the hordes of tourists who descend annually on Cornwall's local beaches and beauty spots. Such teasing is first recorded in print in the 1970s, but it was very likely around somewhat earlier than that.

See also GROCKLE

empt

to pour tea (Somerset)

A shortened form of **empty**, recorded across the South with reference to all sorts of drinks but also in Somerset with specific reference to tea, **empt** has been used for a number of senses of empty since Anglo-Saxon times. The association with the pouring out of a drink, though, is distinctive to the southern dialect use. **Ent**, meanwhile, is a variant found in Cornwall and shares the same history.

See KETTLE'S ON, p. 185, *and also* BIRLE, HELL, MASH, MASK, SCALD, SOAK, TEEM, WET

ennog
alleyway (Liverpool)

Ennog is one of two alternatives Liverpudlians have at their disposal to describe an alleyway, the other being **jigger**. Ennog describes a small urban alleyway between buildings, and is probably a diminutive form of **entry**, with -og being a variant of the suffix -ock (as in hillock).

See BY THE WAY, p. 126, *and also* ENTRY, GINNEL, JIGGER, LOAN, LOKE, SNICKET, TWITCHEL

entry
alleyway (Scotland, the North and Midlands)

Entry has meant 'the entrance to a building' and, by extension, 'a gate or door' since the fourteenth century, but what distinguishes the local entries in Scotland, the Midlands and the north of England from those in standard English is that they don't lead into anything. They are simply alleys leading between houses from one place to another. The transfer of use probably arose from alleyways which had the doors or entrances of a number of houses running off them. The stereotypical back-alleys of terraces are a good example.

See BY THE WAY, p. 126, *and also* ENNOG, GINNEL, JIGGER, LOAN, LOKE, SNICKET, TWITCHEL

fash

bother, fuss (Scotland, northern England and the Lake District)

'Dun't fash thisel,' they say in the Lake District, and a good few places besides (in Scotland it's 'dinna . . .') and what it means is 'don't worry, don't bother yourself'. The word is a direct borrowing from France, where *fâcher* means 'to annoy or to irritate', although the altruistic meaning that underpins our **fash**, 'to bother oneself' (for someone else's sake), doesn't appear to be there. Fash gives **fasherie** (which also offers a very French feel), meaning 'annoyance', and **fashious**, 'troublesome'. Scotland's phrase **never fash yer heid** or **thumb** means 'pay no heed' to such-and-such.

fernticle

a freckle (Scotland and Northern Ireland)

Fernticle, a word thought to be obsolete but recorded by the BBC during its interviews for the Voices Project, is part of older Northern Irish dialect and is also found in Scots as **fairnitickle**. The word originated in the Middle English word **farntikylle**, describing a mark on the skin resembling the seed of the fern.

fettle

condition; state; to clean (Scotland and northern England)

Cleanliness, it seems, remains out there ahead of godliness, at least when it comes to that popular indicator of good condition, being in fine fettle. Indeed, it may all probably go back to standard English **fit**, which has possible links with **fettle**'s own more immediate origin, the Anglo-Saxon word fettle, meaning 'to gird up'. So you can be fettled or girded up (literally speaking, with a gird or belt around one's waist) and so in good condition. Today's verb **to fettle** means 'to clean', 'to tidy', 'to put to rights', while as a noun it denotes a condition, state, order or repair. A **fettler** is a cleaner, and **fettling day** cleaning day.

fitty

good; suitable; correct (Cornwall)

If you are **fitty** in Cornish, you will also be **viddy** in Devonian, and in both places you would be doing the right thing, for both terms mean 'appropriate', 'correct', and hence 'trim and neat'. Both too are probably derived from the now obsolete adjective **featish**, which was used to describe people who were well proportioned or handsome. In the olden days, to behave **fitty-ways** was the ultimate in good etiquette.

fitty-looking

pretty (the South-West and South Wales)

Fitty is recorded in southern speech going right back to the sixteenth century, meaning 'right, proper': the same as the standard English words fit or fitting. By the eighteenth century, it had become strongly focused in the South-West, especially Devon and Cornwall, and a series of extended senses are recorded there too, including 'neat and tidy', 'clever', 'healthy' (the modern sense of fit) and 'attractive, pretty'. The Dorset dialect poems of William Barnes mention 'the vittiest maid in all the feair' (the use of 'v' for 'f' in stressed syllables is characteristic of broad South-West dialect; **feair** means 'fair'). **Fitty-looking** is also common in this sense, especially in 'a fitty-looking maid'.

Fitty continues to be used in the core sense of 'proper' (in the Poldark novels of Winston Graham, for example), and so does fitty-looking.

See SITTING PRETTY, below, *and also* BONNY

Sitting pretty

When it comes to the lexicon of local adjectives for attractive, the cupboard is particularly bare. Half of them rely on a simple pattern whereby a general adjective of approval is combined with -looking. And most of the exceptions are just an adjective of this kind simply used in a specific context, like **braw**, **canny** or **grand**. **Decent**, in Yorkshire, is barely even an adjective of approbation. Compare that with the national adjectives fit, gorgeous, hot, lush, tasty, stonkin, purdy and, of course, sexy.

But there are some older words which still hold their own, including **bonny**, which resembles sexy in that it can nowadays be applied to pretty much anything approved of, and **fitty-looking**, which offers an interesting comparison with the modern **fit**. You may also encounter **bon** (Cumbria), **bonny-looking** (Yorkshire), **bostin** (West Midlands), **braw** (Scotland), **canny** (Cumbria), **decent** (Yorkshire), **fine** (North), **flash**, (Yorkshire), **flasher** (as a noun, Berkshire), **good-like**, **grand, grand-looking** (Yorkshire), **handsome, handsome-looking** (East Anglia), **smart** (more common in the South), **smartish** (Somerset) and **smart-looking** (Kent, Westmorland, Yorkshire).

A nice enough list, but it is strangely small compared to our labels for ugliness. Go figure.

See also BONNY, FITTY-LOOKING

---

flim

five-pound note (Liverpool)

> **Flim** is short for **flimsy**, which refers to paper, specifically that on which currency notes are printed – in this caser a fiver. While the term is currently associated with Liverpool, it dates to the mid-nineteenth century when it apparently had no local ties. Flimsy, some forty years older, was the monetary opposite of another term, **blunt**, which referred to coins.

fluthered

drunk (Ireland)

> Recorded in Ireland from the early twentieth century, **fluthered** can also be found (if sparsely) recorded in the North. Like **stocious**, it is now most often used adverbially as in **fluthered drunk**.

> *See* LIQUID LUNCHES, p. 70, *and also* BLOOTERED, DRUCKEN, DRUFFEN, MAL-LETED, PISHED, PUGGLED, SKIMMISHED, STOCIOUS

fond

silly (Yorkshire)

> **Fond** has been a northern word for hundreds of years, as the past participle of **fon**, an old verb meaning 'to act foolishly' and commonly found in medieval mystery plays from York, Wakefield and Coventry as well as in Shakespeare. It was recorded in Scotland and throughout the North and Midlands in the nineteenth century, but by the time of the Survey of English Dialects, which collected local vocabulary in the 1950s, it had settled mainly in north-east Yorkshire.

> *See* DON'T BE DAFT, p. 89, *and also* ADDLE-HEADED, BARMY, DAFT, GORM-LESS, QUILT, SOFT

fool gowk

April Fool (Scotland and Northumberland)

Gowk is an equivalent to fool (*see* **April gowk**), so **fool gowk** is literally 'fool fool'. It is possible that it was originally part of a reinforcing expression, 'April Fool gowk', and that the April was subsequently dropped. Whatever its origin, though, it retains a strong local flavour for one of the oldest traditions in British culture.

See A PINCH AND A PUNCH, p. 3, *and also* APRIL GAWBY, APRIL GOWK, APRIL NODDY, HUNTIGOWK, MAY GOSLING

forkin robbins

earwig (Yorkshire)

In Latin the earwig is *Forficula auricularis*, which seems to translate as the 'small shears' (*forfix* being the shears part, plus the female diminutive -*ula*) or 'scissors' of the earlobe. The image presumably works better for natural historians. It is, however, that *Forficula* which gives our link to Yorkshire's **forkin robbins**, which also means the common earwig. Where the robbins bit comes from is a mystery: do earwigs have any relationship with the red-breasted bird? According to the *English Dialect Dictionary* it is a very specific term, used in the East Riding of Yorkshire; in the North Riding, or at least in the south of the North Riding, they prefer the term **twitchbell**, which may be a euphemism of another dialectal earwig: the **twitch-ballock**. The **twitch clock** or **twitch clog**, meanwhile, is a cockroach.

freck

to fuss (Cornwall)

To **freck** is, much as it sounds, to fuss. It comes from the word **fraik**, which is defined variously as to flatter, wheedle, cajole, coax and to make much ado about a person in order to gain some object. Thus there is the noun **fraiking**, meaning 'flattering or coaxing', and the adjective freck, describing something or someone wheedling. All that noted, there is yet a further link to consider: the word **freak** in the sense of 'a whim or fancy'. (And freak, which gained such enormous popularity in the days of freak-outs, freaks, and freaky psychedelia, seems, very fittingly, to have its own roots in Anglo-Saxon **fracian**, 'to dance'.)

fuggy

'me first' in children's games (Scotland and the North-East)

Fuggy, used in many a children's game to declare 'I'm first', is one of those terms, like the games themselves, that are far older than our modern world. And while the spelling may have changed, there seems little doubt that it is the modern version of the nineteenth century's **fugie**, **fugie-blow** and **fidgie**, all from the standard English fugitive, which once had another meaning of 'a blow given as a challenge to fight'.

On 30 June 1898, the *Glasgow Herald* ran a long article about fidgies, the ancestors of today's fuggy, which explains them expertly: 'In common use just before the days of School Boards. In those days, as now, it was not always necessary to follow up a challenge with a blow, but the boy who would not fight another of his own size after receiving a "fidjie" was unanimously voted a coward and generally sent to Coventry. When a "fidjie" was not sufficient provocation to produce a fight a second blow was often given, and this couplet repeated: "That's your fidgie, that's your blow; Ye're be't an' I'm no."'

The *Herald* journalist added another word to the mix: 'The more confident of the two combatants usually administered the "foodjie" (a very slight push with the open hand). If his opponent failed to respond to it, then he repeated the following rhyme: "There's the foodjie, there's the blow; Fight me, or else no." The blow was simply another slight push on the breast, but with the closed fist.'

It's not for nothing that the children's playground is seen as one of the most productive generators of new words.

fustilugs

a person of foul habits (Yorkshire)

> In addition to the above, the *Oxford English Dictionary* gives the
> alternative definition of a **fustilugs** as a 'fat, frowzy woman'.
> Whatever their gender, a fustilugs is always someone who is slow
> and heavy (the lug part), with habits that are at best unpleasant and
> at worst positively foul (fusty conjures up smells of damp, mould,
> staleness and a definite lack of freshness). A work from the 1620s
> includes the wonderful line 'Every lover admires his mistress,
> though she be . . . a vast virago, or . . . a fat fustylugs.' Today's
> Yorkshireman may not share quite the same view.

fusty

ugly (London)

> Most of us know **fusty** as something that gives off a stale smell
> (from **fust**, 'a mouldy wine-barrel'). Used of people, however, fusty
> has also meant 'ill-tempered' (at least in Samuel Pepys's diaries),
> 'seedy' and 'smelly', for centuries. Ugliness, its latest meaning, is
> just one step on in its history.

> *See* THE MIRROR CRACKED, p. 31, *and also* BUTTERS, DUFFY, LAIDLY, MING-
> ING, MUNTER, OBZOCKY, RANK, SKANK

g

gadgie

a man (Romany)

Gadjo is the Romany term for any man other than a Gypsy: in other words an alien or outsider. The female form is **gadji**, the plural **gadje**. Gadgie is an alternative spelling, and can, outside Romany circles, be used to mean 'a man', irrespective of ethnicity.

gaffer

a term of respect, or used simply as a term of address (London and the North)

Gaffer, and its female synonym **gammer**, are probably shortened versions of godfather and godmother. Originally, it was a term applied to an elderly man, or one whose position entitled him to respect. In the seventeenth and eighteenth centuries it was the usual prefix, in rustic speech, added to the name of a man below the rank of those addressed as Master. In the nineteenth century, it took on the meaning that we are most familiar with today: 'the foreman or boss of a group of workers'.

gall

blister (the South-West)

> Originally an Anglo-Saxon term denoting a sore or pustule specifically on a horse, **gall** is also used in the South-West to mean 'a callous', and outside the South-West to mean 'a sore place' in general.
>
> **Galling** comes from just that route, the verb gall that is described wonderfully in a seventeenth-century publication as 'to gall, fret, itch; also, to rub, scrape, scrub, claw, scratch where it itcheth'.
>
> *See* THERE'S THE RUB, below, *and also* BLEB, BLISH

There's the rub

It is not unusual to find words whose various dialect synonyms are linked together by alliteration. One example is provided by words for a rung of a ladder, such as **staff**, **stale**, **stap**, **stave** and **stab**. Blister is another. The word **blister** itself appears at the end of the fourteenth century, and **blob** a century later in Scotland. Subsequently, we have **bleb**, **blish**, **blibe**, **blush**, **blaster** and **bladder** (in Cornwall and Devon) and **blaster** (in Hampshire) to name but seven. One suggestion for the ultimate origin of these bl- words is that they imitate the shape of the lips making a bubble (and it's certainly true that many of these words also have the meaning of 'bubble').

Alternatives not beginning with bl- are fairly rare – the most prominent of them being **gall** – but there does appear to have been a wider range before the twentieth century which have since sadly died out. For example, there were **jags** in the North-East, **ercles** in Shropshire and Worcestershire, **flish** in Yorkshire, **glob** and **plish** in Westmorland and **gligs** in Lincolnshire. All of which make good noises of the tongue, even if the thing they describe is to be avoided at all costs.

See also BLEB, BLISH, GALL

gallus

bold; mischievous (Scotland)

Given **gallus**'s somewhat sinister origins, it's at first glance curious that the word has come to mean 'bold, daring' or 'mischievous', especially since the term is usually applied to children. And yet it does, and there is a logic to it. The original term is **gallows**, found as an adjective around 1425 and meaning 'fit for the gallows', 'deserving to be hanged', 'villainous' and 'wicked'. Three hundred years later it had reversed its role – in a progress that can be found repeatedly in slang where bad is so often adopted to mean good – to be used as a general intensifier, denoting 'very great, excellent'.

As a postscript to the story of the word, both gallus and **gallowses** take us today to Scotland and also America, where both terms refer to what Americans call suspenders and what the British call braces. Again descending firmly from the hanging gallows, the apparatus of judicial death, these modern-day versions hang cloth rather than human flesh: you can just picture a rural farmer, his overalls suspended by a single strap.

gammerstang

a tall, awkward woman (Yorkshire and the North; Scotland).

The word **gammer** was once a rustic term for an old woman, and is probably a corruption of grandmother (the male equivalent was **gaffer**). A **stang**, meanwhile, simply means 'a pole'. In some places in Scotland and the north of England, someone who has somehow incurred the indignation of his or her fellow-villagers is compelled to **ride the stang** (either personally, in effigy, or by proxy), accompanied by a jeering crowd and sometimes, according to the *Oxford English Dictionary*, 'rough music'. There is also a New Year's day custom by which every one met by the mob has either to ride the stang or pay a forfeit. Related words are **gomerel**, meaning 'simpleton', and **gamphrel** ('blockhead').

ganny

grandmother (Cumbria)

Ganny has been common in Cumbria and northern Lancashire since the nineteenth century. It is probably a localised version of **gammer**, a word for an old woman (and sometimes specifically a grandmother) that has in turn been recorded since the sixteenth century. **Gammy** emerged in Yorkshire at the same time, but doesn't seem to have had the same staying power. Although the change from -mm- to -nn- is a common pattern, it seems quite likely that the influence of **nanny** is also at play with the development of ganny.

See OH MAI, p. 148, *and also* GRAMMER, MAI, NAIN/NIN

garms

threads, clothes (London and the South-East)

Garms is a term short for garments and, although dating back to Old London, is still in use by the capital's teenagers today. Garms that are **buff** and **criss** (cool and stylish, or **rude**) are of course the best (or **nang**).

garyboy

an ostentatious teenager who drives a souped-up car (East Anglia)

This playfully derogatory term for a boy who drives a 'pimped' car with an extra-loud exhaust and even louder stereo system emerged in the 1990s.

gelt

money (Yorkshire, now rare)

Gelt derives from the German and Dutch *geld*. It was first recorded in the 1520s, in the works of the poet John Skelton, and remained in general English use from then on in. In Yorkshire, especially in the nineteenth century, it came to be widely used in cases where the money in question is the profit from a specific enterprise. In the words of one egg-seller from Swaledale in the 1870s: 'over went my egg-basket; so there wern't much gelt out of that.'

See MONEY TALKS – OR DOES IT?, p. 144, and also ACKERS, MORGS, REVITS, SPONDULICKS

Geordie

a person from Tyneside; the Tyneside dialect (UK-wide)

The home of the **Geordie** depends very much on who is using the term. It can be the whole of England's North-East, the area on the banks of the river Tyne or simply the city of Newcastle. But not Sunderland, where the nickname for its inhabitants is **mackem**. And definitely not Teesside, whose people are otherwise known as **Smoggies**.

No one knows for sure how the term Geordie came about, although everyone agrees it is a version of George, which was popular throughout England in the nineteenth century and the time that the term is first recorded, and particularly so for eldest sons born in the North-East. The *Oxford English Dictionary*'s first finding of it is from 1866 (although some collectors of dialect can pre-date that, and it is almost certain that the word was around in spoken English long before then). The *OED* quotes a publication that states that 'The sailors belonging to the ports on the north-eastern coast of England are called Jordies.' Six years later, the standard spelling had definitely taken over. At almost exactly this time, records show that the mining community of the North-East called pitmen Geordies, because of their use of George Stephenson's safety lamp, which strongly suggests this as a source for modern Geordies.

There are other theories, however, including one well-established one that Newcastle was the home to support of George II during the Jacobite Rebellion of the eighteenth century.

Whatever its origin, Geordies speak with what has been called, following one newspaper's national poll, 'the most attractive accent in England'. As for their unique vocabulary, the wonderfully rich Geordie dialect is rooted in Old English, thanks to the North-East's Anglo-Saxon settlers.

See also MACKEM

ginnel

alleyway (the North-West)

> This is the predominant word in the North-West for a narrow passage between buildings, to be found in Lancashire and West Yorkshire, and also in Cumbria and Cheshire. It is first recorded in a deposition to a Manchester court as far back as 1669. The pronunciation is 'jinnel' in some areas and 'ginnel' in others.
>
> *See* BY THE WAY, p. 126, *and also* ENNOG, ENTRY, JIGGER, LOAN, LOKE, SNICKET, TWITCHEL

glaikit

senseless, foolish, flighty (Scotland and northern England)

> Scotland's **glaikit** means 'stupid', 'foolish', and in later use 'thoughtless', 'flighty', or 'giddy' (stereotypically of a woman). Where it comes from remains unresolved: **glaik**, meaning 'mocking deception' (not to mention 'a flash of light' or 'a child's toy or puzzle'), and used in such phrases as **give** or **play** [someone] **the glaiks** ('to cheat or swindle') and to **get the glaik(s)** ('to be cheated or deceived'), would fit perfectly. Unfortunately though, **glaikit**, at least on present records, looks to be older. Another suggestion sees a link to **gleek**, a jibe or jest, or a coquettish glance. The jury is most definitely still out.

gobslotch

a glutton; an idle fellow (Yorkshire)

> The **gob**, meaning the mouth and now considered vulgar in standard English, retains in dialect the sense it has had since the sixteenth century of 'a lump or large mouthful of food', especially of raw, coarse or fat meat. The slotch element of the wonderfully onomatopœic **gobslotch** is a rewriting of **slouch**, and so a gobslotch was also an idle, slouching fellow: a position resulting perhaps from the state of lethargy induced by too many **gobbets** (another term for those pieces of raw flesh).

Don't be daft

Silly originally described someone who was deserving of pity, sympathy or compassion. It was not until the sixteenth century (over 100 years after its first appearance) that the word took on its main modern meanings of 'foolish' (lacking in judgement) and 'stupid' (weak in intelligence).

Attributing softness to silly people has been a repeated metaphor, with **soft** itself recorded from the seventeenth century. Others containing an element of that same metaphor include **soapy**, **batchy**, **cakey** and even **barmy**. It is present as well in the use of **pudding** to denote a silly person (common from the late eighteenth century). **Daft** is by far the most common alternative to silly, although barmy, **gormless** and **soft** all have their own areas of prominence.

There is a considerable range of registers among the less commonly recorded synonyms. For example, **feckless** in Lancashire sounds a lot more negative than **daffy** in Berkshire. The level of stupidity implied can vary too in line with the dual foolish/stupid meaning. People who are **nutty** or **loopy** may simply be silly in their behaviour, whereas someone who is **half-sharp** may not be able to help it. The wonderful **dateless** in Yorkshire suggests a person who doesn't know what day of the week it is (compare to **Wednesday-and-Thursday**, *see* NO MEAN FEET, p. 62).

But what a lexicon silliness provides. Roam the country and you can find a host of terms for it – some benevolent, some warmly affectionate and others downright despairing. You might, then, hear **addled** (Sussex), **batchy** (Essex), **batty** (South-East), **cakey** (Staffordshire and Shropshire), **cranky** (Midlands), **daffy** (Berkshire), **dafty** (Somerset), **dappy** (Essex), **dateless** (Yorkshire), **dibby** (Lincolnshire), **dozy** (North), **feckless** (Lancashire), **gaumy** (Staffordshire), **gawky** (South-West), **gone** (Somerset), **half-cracked** (Somerset), **half-sharp** (Huntingdonshire), **kimit** (Hertfordshire), **loony** (East Anglia), **loopy** (South-East), **noggen** (Cheshire), **nutty** (Lincolnshire, Sussex), **potty** (South Midlands), **puddled** (Sussex), **queer** (Somerset), **rooky** (South-East), **soapy** (London), **touched** (South-East) or **wappy** (Leicestershire).

See also ADDLE-HEADED, BARMY, DAFT, FOND, GORMLESS, QUILT, SOFT

gormless

silly (Lancashire)

Gormless derives from an Old Norse word *gaumr* meaning 'care, heed'. It is first recorded in the mid-eighteenth century in Lancashire, but subsequently moved out to West Yorkshire, Westmorland and across the North Midlands. The early dialect evidence is in the form **gaumless** (or **gawmless**), including a use in *Wuthering Heights*, and gormless appears to be a respelling as the word passed into general informal English at the end of the nineteenth century. Gormless retains, however, cultural connotations of the industrial North and of its speech, as in Stan Barstow's play *Joby*: 'She's bloody gormless enough to imagine owt.'

See DON'T BE DAFT, p. 89, *and also* ADDLE-HEADED, BARMY, DAFT, FOND, QUILT, SOFT

gowk

a fool (Scotland and northern England)

Like a number of terms that equate an animal and its stereotyped characteristics with humans and their way of life, **gowk** was originally a term for a cuckoo, but it went on to mean 'a fool or awkward person'. Whether the foolishness goes with the bird's notorious nestlessness, it's hard to say, but certainly cuckoo itself has meant 'mad' or at least 'eccentric' for some time. The dialect version of gowk, meanwhile, has given rise to a number of compounds: **to give the gowk to**, 'to fool someone'; **to hunt the gowk**, 'to go on a fool's errand', and the resonant **gowk's-storm**, 'a springtime storm'. **Gowk-thropple** (a thropple being the throat) is an imaginative name for bad language.

See also A PINCH AND A PUNCH, p. 3, *and also* APRIL GOWK, FOOL GOWK

grammer

grandmother (the South, especially the South-West)

Having exactly the same geographical spread, **grammer** clearly forms a pair with **granfer**. In the nineteenth century, **grammy** is recorded in Oxfordshire and Somerset, and seems similarly to parallel **granfy**. It has also been collected by researchers in Lincolnshire, which again fits with the evidence for granfer.

See OH MAI, p. 148, *and also* GANNY, GRANFER, MAI, NAIN/NIN

grammersow

a woodlouse; a millipede (Cornwall)

This colourful term seems to have originated as a joke among the young, for while **grammer** in many counties has meant 'mire' or 'dirt', in Cornwall, where **grammersow** belongs, it has long meant 'grandmother'. The louse is probably being referred to as a grandmother's pig or sow – the idea being she is too old and frail to look after the real thing.

gramp

grandfather (the South)

Although **gramp** is now widely used across Britain, especially in its plural form **gramps**, it first arose in the south-west Midlands, recorded in the *English Dialect Dictionary* of 1902 in Gloucestershire, Oxfordshire and Wiltshire. Half a century later, during the Survey of English Dialects at Leeds University, its range had widened naturally to include the neighbouring counties of Berkshire, Buckinghamshire, Monmouthshire and Northamptonshire. You can also find it in Liverpool. It is, very simply, a shortening of grandpapa.

See 'GRANDAD, GRANDAD . . .', p. 93, *and also* GRANFER, GRANSHER, GUTCHER, TAID

granfer

grandfather (the South, chiefly the South-West)

> **Granfer** (or **grandfer** or **gramfer** or **granfy**) is the dominant
> informal form of grandfather in the south of England, and has been
> since the middle of the nineteenth century. It is particularly
> associated with the South-West; one of the characters in Thomas
> Hardy's *Far from the Madding Crowd* is described as 'his grandfer's
> own grandson'. The same formation has also been recorded, usually
> as **granfa** or **grandfa**, in Lincolnshire, Norfolk and south
> Nottinghamshire. **Grammer** is an exact parallel or pair, meaning
> 'grandmother'.
>
> *See* 'GRANDAD, GRANDAD . . .', p. 93, *and also* GRAMP, GRANSHER, GUTCHER,
> TAID

gransher

grandfather (mid-west England and south-east Wales)

> An informal form of grandsire, **gransher** is recorded in south-east
> Wales and in the counties of England close to the Welsh border,
> such as Gloucestershire and Shropshire.
>
> *See* 'GRANDAD, GRANDAD . . .', p. 93, *and also* GRAMP, GRANFER, GUTCHER,
> TAID

'Grandad, Grandad ...'

The history of dialect words for grandfather is for the most part the history of shortenings, informal uses and pet forms of standard words. Of these standard words, grandfather is not, in fact, the earliest. That title goes to grandsire, which is recorded at the beginning of the fourteenth century, over a hundred years before the first occurrence of grandfather. In Scotland, the altered form **goodsire** became the standard form over the course of the fifteenth century. Both of these terms have now all but disappeared from standard English, but retain a presence in regional English precisely in shortened, informal versions, such as **gransher** and **gutcher**. This kind of variation on grandfather is visible from the eighteenth century, with grandpa, grandpapa, grandpappy and grandpop all emerging by the end of the nineteenth. Most of these terms are now part of general informal language and have lost any regional affiliation they might once have had: grandpa, for example, seems once to have had a strong association with East Anglia.

There are, however, a bevy of local alternatives that persist: **granda** (the North), **granfer** (South-West), **gransher** (South Wales), **bamper** (Glamorgan), **granfy** (Somerset and Gloucestershire), **grampy** (South Midlands), **grand** (Wiltshire), **granda** (Scotland and the Isle of Man), **grandaddy** (Scotland and Northern Ireland), **grandayer** (Isle of Man), **grandpap** (Warwickshire), **grandpop** (Kent), **grandy** (Scotland), **granf** (Somerset), **pap**, **pappy** (Northamptonshire), **pawpie** (Scotland), **pop** (Berkshire and **tadcu** (south-west Wales).

The undoubted king of all grandfatherly names is grandad. It is first recorded in 1793 in Mrs Pilkington's novel *Rosina*, in which one character worries he 'might be caught napping like old grandad'. This date might seem surprisingly late for a word of such obvious derivation, but regular use of familiar words was uncommon in writing before the nineteenth century, so the exact age of those words is often difficult to document.

All in all it's quite a list. Grandfathers have clearly been worthy of note.

See also GRAMP, GRANFER, GRANSHER, GUTCHER, TAID

How to talk like ... **the Cornish**

The problem with all West Country speech is that unless you're a local, the sound you're probably most familiar with is some very, *very* distant ooh-arr approximation to a real south-western accent gleaned from radio or television. Some heavily rolled (rhotic) 'r' sounds, talk of 'zydeRR' and 'vaRRmers', and it seems that it's job done. But that's just what people disparagingly refer to as 'Mummerset'.

The truth about West Country talk is, of course, a great deal more complicated, and there's pretty well as much variation from Camborne to Chewton Mendip as there is from West Lothian to Wick. Of these West Country sounds, the least-heard nationally yet most distinctive are those of Cornish. And sadly for those who get all sentimental about the loss of the older, richer forms of accented British speech, you have to look rather harder these days to find the real clotted cream of a Cornish accent.

Recent surveys have shown massive dilution of the accent among young Cornishmen and women, and a tendency to adopt some of the far-from-local characteristics of vernacular English. Most notable is what linguists call 'TH-fronting', or in layman's terms the use of 'v' to represent the 'th' in words like *mother* and *father*. Today 'muvver' is no longer alien to Cornish mouths and even an elderly man and otherwise very pure dialect speaker was recorded not so long ago pronouncing *with another* as 'wiv anuvver'. Old Cornish speech, along with the vocabulary to match, is usually found among the elderly inhabitants of the villages, close to the land, to the former tin industry and the (still just surviving) china clay business, and of course on the boats of the dwindling Cornish fishing fleet.

But when you hear it, there's no mistaking it: crunchy voiced consonants abound ('v' for 'f', 'z' for 's' – and yes, they do indeed talk of 'vaRRms' for *farms* and 'zydeRR' for *cider*); but they also talk of 'vuzz' for *gorse* (local pronunciation of the old word 'furze') and in the olden, more purely agricultural days, of 'drash' for *thresh*. You get the picture.

Cornish vowels, just like the consonants, are pretty mobile, so the long 'i' in *life* becomes more of an extended 'ah' sound – 'maah laaf' (for *my life*), 'skaavin'' (*skiving* – playing truant) and 'samdaams' (*sometimes*). And this is nothing new. All of 400 years ago, a nobleman from London, Richard Carew, reported in a famous compendious volume on the state of Cornwall, including a section on the way the locals spoke there in 1602. So, in a sort of audio time capsule that's been passed down to us, we can read that the locals have 'a broad and rude accent . . . specially in pronouncing the names: as Thomas they call, *Tummas*, Matthew, *Mathaw*: Nicholas, *Nichlaaz*, David, *Daavi*: Mary, *Maari* . . .'

Elsewhere among classic Cornish vowels, the 'ow' sound in *our* is sharpened to 'aar' – they talk of 'aRR language'; and as for the long 'oo' sound that crops up in *move*, *dilute*, *cool* and so on, this among older and more traditional speakers emerges as a complicated cocktail of sounds with elements of 'a', 'u' and 'y' in it – 'muyve', 'dahluyte' and 'cuyl' would be some sort of approximation.

But true Old Cornish speech also uses 'thee' and 'thou' (often elided with the preceding syllable to become simple 'ee'. ''Ere's lookn at 'ee, maid' would have been Bogey's famous remark in a Cornish-language version of *Casablanca*). Also being eroded in the fast-fire snap and crackle of true Cornish is the little word 'it' – 'it is' and 'it was' readily turn into 'tis' and 'twas'. And this chopping-out of syllables is a real feature of the accent. That lovely local term 'directly' meaning something like the Spanish *mañana* (but, as the old joke goes, without the same sense of urgency!) is always pronounced 'dreckly'. There was even once a famous local bumper sticker announcing 'Cornish People Do It Dreckly'.

And nowhere more than in the county's place names, embedded in the landscape by years of highly local speech, are such eroded forms to be found. So Launceston is 'Lanson' (and 'like Lanson Gaol' is an old dialect expression for describing a mess or a muddle), Fowey is 'Foy' and St Austell 'Snaazl'.

In Cornwall you're quite likely to be greeted as **me 'ansum** (my handsome), still a regular form of address or affection. **Ansum** or **'andsome** is Cornish for *beautiful* or *fine*. Unless, that is, you're an **emmet** (ant), used to refer to incomers or tourists, tolerated for their money-spending propensities. Among the older generation, at least, a girl or daughter is a **maid**, and something that's good or appropriate is often **fitty**. If the **tacker** (child) is **squallin'** (crying) it's maybe just because she's irritable or **teasy**. If you're rude, though, you're likely to be called **forthy**, just the sort of thing to make someone **mazed** (annoyed); on the other hand, maybe you're just **rigged up** (excited). Time perhaps to calm yourself down with a bite to eat – your **croust** (packed lunch) is in your bag, and consists of **tiddy oggie** (potato pasty). If you don't, you run the risk of ending up **wisht as a winnard** (sick as a redwing).

SIMON ELMES

griggles

small worthless apples left on a tree (Wiltshire)

A **grig**, in the fifteenth century, was a diminutive person or thing, while a **grig-hen** in some counties is still the preferred term for a short-legged hen. This sense of smallness may be the source of **griggles**, which are the small apples left on the tree by the picker as they are too little to be of any value.

grockle

tourist (the West Country)

The term **grockle** originated in the West Country, specifically in Torbay, where a local once supposedly remarked that the stream of visitors to the town resembled 'little Grocks' – a reference to the celebrated nineteenth-century Grock the clown, real name Charles Adrien Wettach. Soon it spread throughout Britain's holiday resorts where the local people used to deride the flocks of annual visitors to their area. The term was never fully popularised until the making, in 1962, of the film *The System* (starring Oliver Reed and Barbara Ferris and otherwise known as *The Girl-Getters*). As explained by etymologist Michael Quinion, 'the word was popularized because of its use in the film, the script-writer having picked the word up from the locals during filming in Torquay.'

Further research by a local journalist in the mid-1990s linked the word 'to a strip cartoon in the comic *Dandy* entitled "Danny and his Grockle"', in which the grockle was a magical dragon-like creature. A local man, who had had a summer job at a swimming pool as a youngster, said that he had used the term as a nickname for a small elderly lady who was a regular customer one season. During banter in the pub among the summer workers, the term then became generalised as an expression for summer visitors. It's probably a safe bet that this anecdote marginally preceded the making of the movie, but it is thanks to the film that grockles are now truly out there (much to the locals' disgust).

See also EMMET

grouts

sediment at the bottom of a cup or glass (Cornwall)

> **Grouts** (also known as **groushans** in West Cornwall) refer to any
> form of gritty sediment, including the lees (or dregs) of wine or
> beer, or the deposits left at the bottom of a cup of tea or coffee.
> While it is related to the material that DIY-ers put between tiles in its
> consistency and its etymology, its application is very different,
> certainly in the context of declaring that something can be 'as sweet
> as grout', in other words like the last part of a cup of tea, with the
> sugar left unstirred at the cup-bottom.
>
> Grout comes from Anglo-Saxon **grut**, which in turn corresponds
> to the Middle Dutch word *grute* or *gruit*, meaning 'coarse meal',
> 'peeled barley or rye', 'malt', 'flavouring for beer', or 'yeast'. It was
> first recorded around 725. Thus many of the original uses of the
> word referred to beer: either to new ale, weak or second-rate small
> beer (once drunk rather than water, and by all ages and at any time
> of the day, hence the idiom), or to **grout-ale**, which was sweet,
> heady ale. A **grouter** was an inn-keeper, and a **grout-night** a feast
> at which all enjoyed themselves thanks to the consumption of
> grout-ale. The sole party-pooper is the Shetlands where grout
> refers not to ale, but to the refuse of fish livers after the oil has been
> melted out. Not quite so tasty.

gurt

great; good (the South-West and particularly Bristol)

> **Gurt**, or its counterpart **girt**, can be heard in Bristol from the
> mouths of both young and old. It is a simple twist on great, and is an
> all-purpose term of approval which can precede virtually any
> adjective or noun.

gutcher

grandfather (Scotland now rare)

Gutcher is a word that has recently become rare having been common in Scotland for four centuries. It began life in the early 1500s as a variant of **goodsire**, a Scottish equivalent of grandsire; goodsire is first recorded in the fifteenth century and it too continued in common use until the early decades of the twentieth, after which it fell out of use. Gutcher was also recorded in the north of England in the nineteenth century by Louis Lucien Bonaparte, the nephew of Napoleon, who was born in England after his parents were arrested at sea by the Royal Navy and who went on to become one of the most prolific of all collectors of British dialect words.

See 'GRANDAD, GRANDAD . . .' p. 93, *and also* GRAMP, GRANFER, GRANSHER, TAID

gutties

gym shoes worn in schools (Scotland and Northern Ireland)

Few items evoke such strong memories of primary schools as the sight of a geometry set, a tub of PVA glue or a pair of **plimsolls**, **daps** or **gutties**. Made of black canvas and vulcanised rubber, gutties are still used in primary schools today. Used in Scotland, it is believed that the name is a contraction of *gutta-percha*, the Malay term for India-rubber.

In parts of Scotland, **guttie** is used to refer to other items made of rubber, ranging from golf balls (**guttie ba**) to catapults.

See ANYONE FOR SANNIES? p. 99, *and also* DAPS, PUMPS, SANNIES

Anyone for sannies?

Word-lovers are not used to looking at shoes to fulfil their interest (any more than shoe fetishists are used to looking at words). Boots and shoes have never been terribly productive of colourful local synonyms. But the soft, rubber-soled PE shoe has enough variation on its own to make up for the lack of interest found elsewhere. The fact that there is no clear standard term helps in creating diversity. Gym shoes would be a neutral term, but while everyone would understand, not many would actually use it.

Plimsoll is the nearest thing to a standard, and is the dominant term in the South-East. It is found along the south coast as far west as Exeter, up through Berkshire, Bedfordshire and East Anglia, and in eastern Lincolnshire as far north as Grimsby. It also has an interesting etymology: it is named after Samuel Plimsoll, the Derby MP who introduced the Merchant Shipping Act of 1876, leading to the use of the Plimsoll line to show the safe level to which cargo may be loaded on a merchant ship. Apparently the rubber strip which covers the join between the upper and sole of these shoes reminded people of the Plimsoll line, both in appearance and in its function of ensuring watertightness.

In Scotland, **sandshoe** acts as a standard, which extends into the north-east of England as far south as Hull. The rest of Britain is filled up with a variety of terms ranging from **pumps**, which dominates the North and Midlands, to **gollies**, which is restricted to Merseyside, Cheshire and North Wales. Northern Ireland has the curious **mutton dummies**. Recently more general slang terms for trainers have begun to proliferate, in tune with their greater fashion status. Some of these, such as **kicks** and **runners**, have also been applied to PE footwear, although this may mean no more than that flashy trainers are increasingly being used for PE in place of the traditional plimsoll.

Last on the list, but still very much alive, are **plimmies**, **sneakers** (US in origin), and or **squeakers** (now widespread).

See also DAPS, GUTTIES, PUMPS, SANNIES

hadder

drizzle (Cumbria and Isle of Man)

> **Hadder** is recorded in Durham and North Yorkshire, but more commonly in Cumbria and in the Isle of Man. As one Lake District resident, speaking at the beginning of the twentieth century, had it: 'Nay, it'll rain nin . . . it may hadder a bit.' Its origin is uncertain, but hadder is a common northern form of heather, and heather is likewise recorded in the Lake District as a variant of hadder, so perhaps the suggestion is that the drizzle is like falling heather.
>
> *See* DON'T TALK DRIZZLE, p. 10, *and also* BANGE, MIZZLE, SMIRR

harry hotters

hot (London)

> The interest in the intriguing expression **harry hotters** is less in the hot, which is just what it says on the label, but the long-established combination of harry and -ers. An RAF coinage from the 1940s, **harry** has come to mean 'very', but its origins are less simple. The prevailing view is that the origin lies in the old commercial travellers' phrase **Harry Freemans**, slang for 'free' or 'without charge', which in turn comes from (**drink at**) **Freeman's Quay**, an actual quay near the nineteenth-century London Bridge, where free drinks were handed out to porters and carmen. Why 'free' should become 'very', though, is unclear.

The -ers, meanwhile, is 1920s Oxford slang, where -er was thrown onto anything that would take it (and much that wouldn't), resulting in the **pragger-wagger**, 'the Prince of Wales', and the **wagger-pagger-bagger**, a 'waste-paper basket'. Perhaps the last nationwide survivor is **rugger**, for 'rugby'.

hawch

to eat sloppily (Staffordshire)

Based on the German *hauch*, meaning 'breath' or 'aspiration', to **hawch** means 'to eat badly', usually with much slopping of the lips. To **hoach and haw** is dialect's version of to hawk and spit; a **hawchmouth** is a foul-mouthed blusterer (who one hopes is not eating at the same time), and **hawchmouthed** takes in both senses: being both 'obscene' and, in the context of eating, 'noisy'. The phrase for someone who stands around and does nothing but eat and gossip is one who is **bide and hauchy like a girt** [i.e. great] **fat pig**, a truly punchy expression in which bide means unmoving (as in biding your time).

hedgeboar

hedgehog (the South-West, now rare)

An alternative to hedgehog, **hedgeboars** were, in name, once very common in the South-West. Another local version, **hedgyboar**, was also common, and was around in the 1950s when it was collected in the Survey of English Dialects.

hell

to pour tea (Dorset)

Hell is a Scandinavian word with the general sense of 'pour'. There are records of it in northern English dating back to the fourteenth century, and by the eighteenth it had spread down to the South-West, where it was typically used with reference to the pouring out of drinks, like tea – or cider. The form **hale** is also found.

See KETTLE'S ON, p. 185, *and also* BIRLE, EMPT, MASH, MASK, SCALD, SOAK, TEEM, WET

hoggan

a pasty (Cornwall and the South-West)

Hoggan, properly, means 'pastry' (and as such is probably linked to the Welsh **chwiogen**, 'a muffin or simnel-cake'). Abbreviated to **oggy**, it becomes a form of pasty, a flat cake based on potatoes and originally holding a lump of salt pork in its middle. Such portable snacks are widely popular – they could be taken easily to the field, requiring no fancy ingredients, and can be found across the country. Lincolnshire, for instance, has (or certainly had) its **clanger**, again a pastry wrapping meat (and vegetables) at one end and in this case some form of jam 'for afters' at the other.

The hoggan/oggy can also come as a **figgy hoggan**, in which the salt pork is either replaced by the figs (giving a sort of non-industrialised fig roll), or the figs: like the jam, are stuck at the opposite end. Nor need it always be figs; apples or raisins work just as well. Still in Cornwall, the **hoggan-bag** was a miner's bag in which he carried provisions, although rather than pasties, these were cuts of mutton or beef boiled or baked in a pie crust.

See also CLANGER, OGGY

homie

friend or mate (UK-wide but particularly London and major cities)

Homie has meant 'a person from one's hometown or neighbour-hood' (a homeboy or homegirl), or 'a member of one's peer group or gang', since the 1940s. Earlier still, and in Australia, it was used for a British immigrant newly arrived and still nostalgic for home. However, it is largely thanks to black US hip-hop slang, and in particular to rap, that it is being taken up with such enthusiasm today.

The first quotation for homie in the *Oxford English Dictionary* is from *The Original Handbook of Harlem Jive* (1944), which gives the meaning of 'one newly arrived from the South, a person from one's home-town, one who isn't fully aware of what is going on'. This sense of inexperience has been lost over time, and a homie is now simply a close friend or buddy. If you are hanging with your homies, you are spending time, or 'marinating' ('chilling') with them.

See also BLOOD, BREDREN, BUTTY, CATERCOUSIN, CHUCK, CLICK, CREW, MARRA, MUCKER, SORRY

hookum snivey
a trick or deceit (Devon and the South-West)

This wonderful expression, which also appears as **hook'em snivey** and **hookem-snivvy**, was used on the streets of Victorian London of someone who feigned mortal sickness, disease or infirmity in order to find compassion (and coins) from passers-by. Francis Grose, in his 1811 *Dictionary of the Vulgar Tongue,* defines another form of hookum snivey: 'This rig consists in feeding a man and a dog for nothing, and is carried on thus: Three men, one of who pretends to be sick and unable to eat, go to a public house: the two well men make a bargain with the landlord for their dinner, and when he is out of sight, feed their pretended sick companion and dog gratis.'

The origin of the pithy expression probably lies in the verb hook, as in 'to lure by trickery', and snivey, a word that may once have meant 'deceit' and that may be related to the idea of snivelling. According to a slang dictionary of 1874, the term could also be used as 'an irrelevant answer, as in "Who did that?" "Hook um snivey" – actually no one.'

hoppen

a fair (Scotland and northern England)

> **Hoppen**, from the North-East, means 'a funfair', and appears to combine a pair of monosyllables: hop and ken. The first, **hop**, has meant a dance since the mid-eighteenth century and is based on a variety of northern European roots meaning 'to jump about'. The second, **ken**, was what the *Oxford English Dictionary* terms 'vagabond's slang for a room or place', and most likely comes from the standard English term **kennel** (in a non-canine mode) or from Hindi *khan(n)a*, both of which mean 'a house or room' and which can also be found in combinations such as **buggy-khanna** (coach house), **bottle-khanna** (drinking house), or indeed **gymkhana**, which was once the ball-house or racquet court, a place for athletic sporting events.
>
> One other option is out there: the nineteenth-century slang chronicler J. C. Hotten thought it to be of Romany origin, noting that 'all slang and cant words which end in -ken are partly of Gypsey origin'.
>
> We may never know the truth.

hungered

hungry (Cumbria, Durham and Northumberland)

> **Hungered** functions in the far north of England as a simple version of hungry. Etymologically, it is a survival of the Middle English adjective **a-hungered** with the loss of the weak first syllable, probably under the influence of the past participle of the verb to hunger. In 1803, an important early student of northern dialects, Samuel Pegge, wrote that 'in the north they say of one who keeps his servants on short commons that he hungers them.'
>
> *See* LEERY FOR LUNCH , p. 106, *and also* CLAMMED, CLEMT, LEER/LEERY, YAP

Leery for lunch?

In a reversal of the usual, synonyms for hungry seem more likely to take hold in the South than in the North. The only alternative widely recorded north of the Midlands is **hungered**, which is very close to the standard term anyway. You can be **wallow** in Cumbria and **gant** in Yorkshire, but neither is as common or as widespread as equivalents found in the Midlands and the South, including **famelled** (the south-west Midlands and Oxfordshire), **empty**, **famishing** (Yorkshire and the Midlands), **hearty** (Worcestershire and Surrey), **jimp** (Aberdeen), **pined** (East Midlands) and **sinking** (Sussex).

> *See also* CLAMMED, CLEMT, HUNGERED, LEER/LEERY

huntigowk
April Fool (Scotland)

> In the early eighteenth century, the phrase **to hunt the gowk** was used to mean 'to go on a fool's errand', but by the end of the century it had come primarily to mean 'play an April Fool on someone'. Subsequently, **hunt-the-gowk** became another term for an April Fool, and over the course of the nineteenth century, it was shortened to **huntigowk**, either for April Fool's Day itself, or for the tricks played on it. One 12-year-old girl from Edinburgh told researchers in the 1950s: 'Huntigowk is a day I love. I like to put a basin of water at the side of my sister's bed and hear her let out a yell when she puts her feet into it.'

> *See* A PINCH AND A PUNCH, p. 3, *and also* APRIL GAWBY, APRIL GOWK, APRIL NODDY, FOOL GOWK, MAY GOSLING

izels

pieces of soot or embers from an unswept chimney or a fire (the Isle of Wight and Cumberland)

Once again dialect fills a linguistic gap in standard English; in the case of **izels**, it is for those specks of soot or ash that float through the air while hay or a lit fire is burning.

jackbit

a snack; a packed lunch (the South-West, Berkshire and Hampshire)

Among **bit**'s many meanings is 'a piece of food', thus **jackbit** means 'a bite of something to eat', usually in the morning. (Thus too the older and beautiful **dew-bit**, which is still to be found in Somerset, Dorset, Berkshire and Hampshire, and which means the mid-morning breakfast taken in the fields when the dew is still on the ground.) But why **jack**? Probably because jack is a generic term for a fellow or bloke; more specifically it can also mean 'a young workman', exactly the sort of person to carry such a meal.

See CLOCKING UP YOUR CROUSTS, *p. 214, and also* BAG, BAIT, CLOCKING, NUMMIT, SNAP, TOMMY

jaffock

to gossip (Lancashire)

Jaffock is an imitative formation – you can just hear the movement of the jaw as the chatterer chatters – but perhaps not exactly imitative of gossip or chatter alone, as it is recorded in the nineteenth century in Cheshire meaning 'to argue'. Jaffock defies the dialect dictionaries, but it's possible to offer a guess at its origins. A blend of **jaw**, whether a literal jaw, or in the sense of chatter or gossip, and **fake**, which, before it gained its popular meaning of alter or disguise, meant among eighteenth-century thieves and vagabonds 'to make' (usually for the purposes of deception). So, to borrow an old-fashioned bit of American, **jaffocking** may be 'making with the jaw', just as someone who wags with the chin is a 'chinwag'.

See ALL THE LOCAL GOSSIP, p. 34, and also CANK, CANT, CHAMRAG, CLISH-MA-CLAVER, COOSE, JANGLE, NEIGHBOUR, PROSS, TALE-PYET

jangle

to gossip (Liverpool and North Wales)

Recorded in the fourteenth century with the sense of chattering or babbling, **jangle** is of French origin. It is probably echoic of the noise we're making, and of course it exists in standard English as well as dialect. If, however, the standard jangles are usually metallic objects, the dialect form deals in people, whose jangle is gossip or empty chatter. It is now used chiefly in Liverpool, on Merseyside, and in North Wales both as a verb and as a noun.

There is in fact a host of terms from the same root which turn idle chatter into the angry kind: the verb **to jangle** can mean to quarrel angrily, and so a **janglement** is an angry dispute and a **jangler** a quarrelsome wrangler. **Janglesome** once meant quarrelsome, and a **jangling** can be an argument, generally of the sort that the police term a domestic. Finally, when used of children, the verb means 'to cry'. In all senses the idea is of a noise, and usually an unpleasant one.

The noun use denoting gossiping is especially common in Liverpool, e.g. 'He knew Dave missed all the jangle from Liverpool as much as he did.' This sense was also collected in nineteenth-century Suffolk.

See ALL THE LOCAL GOSSIP, p. 34, *and also* CANK, CANT, CHAMRAG, CLISH-MA-CLAVER, COOSE, JAFFOCK, NEIGHBOUR, PROSS, TALE-PYET

janner

young person in trendy clothes and flashy jewellery (the South-West)

> **Janner** is a regional nickname for inhabitants of Plymouth and their dialect, and by extension someone with a Devon accent. It is thought to be a mocking self-reference to the Devonian pronunciation of the common name John. It is now, however, not quite so harmless, for it has become the equivalent in this area of the South-West to **chav**. This use fits in with the trend of using a colloquial term for a town's residents for a member of that same town's youth subculture (*see* **trobo**).

> *See* THE CHAVS AND THE CHAV-NOTS, p. 43, *and also* CHARVER, CHAV, KAPPA SLAPPER, NED, PIKEY, SCALLY, TROBO

jannicking

messing around (Suffolk)

> **Jannicking** is an old Suffolk term for wasting time, or messing around. This is a little paradoxical, at least in geographical terms, since its root appears to be in **jank**, a term born hundreds of miles away in Scotland and meaning 'to trifle or waste time at work', and, when used as a noun, 'a shuffling trick'. Quite how it travelled to Suffolk while bypassing the north of England remains one of dialect's mysteries. But jannicking, thankfully, looks there to stay.

jannock

fair; straightforward; genuine (UK-wide but particularly Northumberland, Hampshire, Norfolk and Cornwall)

> The origins of **jannock**, which can also be **jonnick**, **jannock** or **jenick**, are frustratingly elusive. Recorded from the early nineteenth century, it can be found across Britain and is very much a thriving modern dialect term. The first quotation in the *Oxford English Dictionary* gives the flavour of it, taken from a dictionary of Craven in the West Riding of the County of York: '"That isn't jannock", i.e. not fair, a phrase in use when one of the party is suspected of not drinking fairly.'

How to talk like... an East Anglian

This, of course, is an impossibility. Ask any Norfolk 'bor' or her Suffolk cousin. East Anglia isn't an amorphous mass of folk who all speak the same way: the accent of Norwich, they'll tell you right enough, is a world away from how they speak down in Ipswich. And yet to the outsider the sound is similar, with a never-to-be-mistaken 'tune' that makes most imitators blanch. I only ever knew one actor (the late Peter Tuddenham) who really could 'do' Norfolk and its combination of idiosyncratic syntax, rich lexicon of local terminology and that rolling, singing melody. This switchback bouncing ride of a tune sweeps the speaker along, de-emphasising some syllables while landing heavily on others and often reducing vowels to mere shadows of their standard selves. So *horses* are 'HAWsis', *knackered* is 'NECKud' and *roast beef*, 'RUSS beef'.

And even if he or she gets the drift, in East Anglia north and south the outsider's sure to get confused by the way the locals systematically switch 'that' for *it*. ''As the fines' fish in tuh'sea, a hairr'n' is . . .' says the old skipper about his favourite fish ('It's the finest fish in the sea, a herring is'). 'Thass my bathday today' ('It's my birthday today') announces another. And so on.

And then there are the vowels. As so often in the dialects of Britain, it's the way the patterns of vowels have shifted round the mouth and taken each other's places that gives an accent its distinctiveness. You have only to hear an 'oo' sound in words containing 'u' to recognise someone's northern-English origins. So in that big lump of flat land bellying out into the North Sea that is East Anglia, the vowels have again swivelled around. *Boats* – and there are many in this watery part of the world – are 'butts', *birthdays* are 'baathdyes' ('ur' rendered as 'aa' and 'ay' as 'eye'), and the 'or' sound found in that bootiful cathedral city of *Norwich* hardens up to a long 'aa'. In consequence its name (benefiting too from the classic East Anglian squeezing of the syllables) routinely becomes simply 'Narge'.

In East Anglia, you suffer not with a bad back, but with a 'bed beck' – the short 'a' tightening towards short 'e', and as we've seen, your *payday* becomes your 'pie-dye' and *eye* in its own standard English right morphs into 'oy' (the 'Oil of Woight' would be a Suffolk visitor's description of the island off Southampton). As for the 'o' sound itself, as heard in the standard pronunciation of 'cold', it inevitably goes walkabout and not consistently so. A recent survey heard the word pronounced to rhyme with *prowled* while 'go' often comes out as 'goo'; and as we've also heard, those ubiquitous Norfolk boats can also be 'butts'.

The glottal stop, so familiar a feature to speakers of London English, indeed crops up here again all across the region. But the Norfolk and Suffolk variety combines it rather attractively with that rollercoaster intonation pattern, and injects just a little microsecond of pause that's just not there in the East End version. The little village of Attleborough is predictably 'A''leborough' but listen to these glottal-stopping whoppers in which *temper*, *jumper* and *knickers* end up sounding more like 'TEM'uh', 'JUUM'uh' and 'NI'az'. Here the glottal is accompanied by a tiny puff of air that helps give the bounce to the tune of East Anglian speech.

On the other hand, completely missing from the gentle loping pattern of the Norfolk and Suffolk accent is the crackle of what's called rhoticity, that is the sounding of 'r's where normally they'd be silent (as in the West Country pronunciation of *father*, *mother*, *butter* and so on).

Oh yes, and if you thought that Bernard Matthews was making up the way he described the quality of his turkeys, think again. 'Bootiful' – or rather 'boo'iful', with a glottal stop instead of a 't' – is standard throughout Suffolk and Norfolk, where the 'you' sound in *news*, *student* and *opportunity* routinely becomes the simpler 'oo': 'noos', 'stoodunt' and 'awpatooni'y'.

But it's when the accent is combined with the rich and often obscure Norfolk and Suffolk vocabulary that the full glory of this most neglected of British accents takes flight: a visit to the outside toilet in an old Norfolk house was to go to the 'petty' ('PEH''y'), you greeted your mate as your 'bor' (from *neighbour*) and started almost every sentence with the expletive 'blust' as in 'Cor blust me!'. If you want to interject into a conversation, you still might want to ask your interlocutor to 'Hold you hard!'

And as for when that east wind comes sweeping in off the North Sea in winter, you could well complain you're **fruz** ('Ahm pairrished fruz') or **frawn** ('Ahm frawn a-cold!'), and you'd greet a female (**mawther**) friend '**Hello, my lil' ole mawther**'; 'little old . . .' is a typical semi-affectionate expression that seems to glue itself to most things you want to tell a story about: '**This lil' ole butt . . .**' (equivalent to 'There was this boat . . .') in this part of the world. And of course, most disparaging remarks would condemn whatever was being moaned about as **squit** (rubbish, nonsense). In Arnold Wesker's classic Norfolk-set play, *Roots*, the central character tries valiantly to persuade her mother that classical music isn't all rubbish; '**Not all on it's squit**,' finally admits the mother.

SIMON ELMES

jay-legged

knock-kneed (Yorkshire and Northumberland)

Like pigeon-toed, the implication of **jay-legged** is that a person has the frail legs of a small bird. Thomas Wilson's Geordie poem *The Oiling of Dicky's Wig* (1843) expresses Dicky's rural contempt for urban visitors in his description of 'the jay-legg'd bodies frae the toon'.

See KNOCK KNOCK, p. 122, *and also* KAY-LEGGED, KNAP-KNEED

jigger

alleyway (Lancashire and Merseyside)

Lancashire's **jigger** means a narrow entry between houses, and is linked to such synonymous terms as **ginnel**. The term also exists in criminal slang, and it is probably among rogues and thieves that it was first used. For them it meant a door (or doorkeeper), a key, a prison (or a cell). Thus the **jigger-dubber** was a turnkey, i.e. a warder, and to **strike a jigger** was either to pick a lock, or failing such skills, to break down a door. The etymology is unknown, but the best guess may be Welsh **gwddor**, a gate. Alternatively it may simply be an alteration of **ginnel**. It is one of the most characteristic Liverpool words. As one **scally** brags in Kevin Sampson's novel *Outlaws*, 'I'm the lad that can get them to perform a sex act in a back jigger.'

See BY THE WAY, p. 126, *and also* ENOG, ENTRY, GINNEL, LOAN, LOKE, SNICKET, TWITCHEL

All paggered and pootled

If you had just finished writing a book on British dialects, you would be **razzored** (if you were from Derbyshire), or **gone in** (if you were from Devon). Wherever you were from, it's likely the word you would use would be a past participle. Sometimes it will be an obvious one, such as done, gone, jaded, worn. Sometimes, as with **jiggered** or **maggled**, it will describe something that you've done or that's been done to you to make you that tired. Sometimes it won't even be clear what the past participle or its verb means (e.g. **faldered**, **paggered**, **wabbit**), but as long as it follows 'I am' and some suitable adverb (totally, utterly, completely, clean, etc.), nobody will be in any doubt as to what you are saying.

Dialect offers a selection of local terms that is anything but weary. They include **bauch** (Scotland), **clammed** (Wiltshire), **defeat** (Scotland), **done in** (South and East Midlands), **done off** (Durham), **done out** (South and Isle of Man), **done up** (chiefly in the South), **faldered** (Lincolnshire, Yorkshire), **fornyward** (Scotland), **gone in** (Devon), **jaded** (Staffordshire), **jaded out** (Yorkshire), **jossed up** (Lancashire), **paggered** (Yorkshire), **paid out** (Yorkshire and North-East), **pootled** (Cumbria), **razzored** (Derbyshire), **bellowsed** (Somerset), **lagged out** (Berkshire), **mucked** (Cheshire), **pegged out** (Westmorland), **played out** (Yorkshire), **pole-fagged** (Lancashire), **spunned up** (Wiltshire), **spun out** (Somerset), **tewed out** (Cumberland), **weared out** (Warwickshire, Devon) and **wore out** (Buckinghamshire).

See also BLETHERED, BUSHWHA, DIRT DEEN, JIGGERED, LAMPERED, MAGGLED, WABBIT

jiggered

tired (Yorkshire, Lancashire and the Midlands)

> Like **wabbit**, **jiggered** (usually with up, as in 'I'm jiggered up') suggests a state of extreme tiredness, almost of being 'done for' and completely devitalised. It may be based on the word jig, although no definitive origin has been traced.
>
> According to the *OED*, jiggered dates back to 1862. It originated

in Yorkshire, and it retains evidence of strong regional use, notably in Lancashire, the Midlands and in Westmorland. It also seems to be common in Scottish English, and features in the works, for example, of the novelists Jeff Torrington and Alan Warner.

Jiggered is also used as a vague substitute for a profane oath or swear-word, as in 'well, I'm jiggered'. In Dickens's *Great Expectations*, Pip reports the labourer Dolge Orlick as saying 'I'm jiggered if I don't see you home.' In this sense, jiggered is probably serving as a euphemism for buggered.

See ALL PAGGERED AND POOTLED, p. 115, *and also* BLETHERED, BUSHWHA, DIRT DEEN, LAMPERED, MAGGLED, WABBIT

jiggery-pokery
underhand practices; manipulation of equipment (Scotland and the North)

The charm of **jiggery-pokery** is such that it often features among Britons' favourite words. Its bouncing rhythm is reminiscent of the language used with a child, working in the same way as higgledy-piggledy does.

The word is first recorded by the *OED* in 1893 as part of a glossary of Wiltshire dialect, but the *English Dialect Dictionary* also quotes an Oxford example: 'I was fair took in with that fellow's jiggery-pokery over that pony.' It very probably comes from an equally onomatopoeic Scots phrase of the seventeenth century, **joukery-pawkery**, in which **joukery** meant 'underhand dealing or deceit', and the whole 'clever trickery' or 'jugglery'. Joukery in turn comes from the verb **jouk**, which once meant to 'dodge' or 'skulk'. Its origin is not proven but it may be linked to the term **jink** and to the American football term **juke**, 'to make a move designed to deceive an opponent'. **Pawky** is a word still in use in northern England, Scotland and Ireland, and means 'artful, sly and shrewd' or, more recently, 'to have a sardonic sense of humour'.

jimp

neat; smart; slender (Scotland and northern England)

A **jimpey** was a short gown worn by a cottage woman. It lacked skirts and reached only the middle of the legs. It is possible that this, which is the root of **jimp** meaning graceful and neat, is in turn linked to the modern **jumper**, which was originally a kind of short coat worn by men in the seventeenth and eighteenth centuries.

joblocks

fleshy, hanging cheeks (Shropshire)

This wonderfully onomatopoeic word says it all. **Joblocks** are the pendulous wattles seen in turkeys and, in human form, the chubby cheeks of a small child or the fat cheeks of an adult. The verb **jobble**, now obsolete, once meant 'moving unevenly like a choppy sea'.

joppety-joppety

nerves or trepidation (Dorset)

This nicely onomatopoeic term comes from the dialect noun **jaup**, which means the breaking of a wave, and thus, more figuratively, a 'shaking up' of something. There is also a verb, **to jaup**, which means 'to splash or to spatter with mud or water'. The word **joppety-joppety** is simply an imitation of the sound reduplicated, representing the jagged spurts of panic. (Jaup, incidentally, is also at the root of Dorset's **jowpment**, a meat stew or hash.)

kappa slapper

a young woman in trendy clothes and flashy jewellery (northern England)

Kappa slapper is the only one of the synonyms and near-synonyms of **chav** (with the exception of **charva**) which specifically denotes a female. It is, however, not so much a regional word as a regional marker. It isn't distinctively used in one region or another, but it is used fairly widely. It *is* often used to designate northerners. All of these features stem from its unusual origin. Kappa Slappa was a short-lived character in the magazine *Viz* (which is produced in Newcastle); she was a young Newcastle woman who lived the life and wore the clothes associated with the urban youth subculture. Her name was based on that of the well-known Italian sportswear company Kappa, plus slapper, slang for 'a promiscuous woman'. She was, in effect, a satirical caricature of a female **charver** and first appeared in the magazine at the end of 1997 (the year that charver is first recorded). The name was changed to Tasha Slappa, apparently after a complaint from Kappa, but by then the genie was out of the bottle. By 1999 the term had been picked up from London to Edinburgh, partly to describe local Kappas, and partly to describe the subculture as a characteristic phenomenon of northern cities.

See THE CHAVS AND THE CHAV-NOTS, p. 43, and also CHARVER, CHAV, JANNER, NED, PIKEY, SCALLY, TROBO

kay-legged

knock-kneed (Yorkshire and Hampshire)

Kay is an old northern word of Scandinavian origin meaning 'left' when used of the left hand or (less commonly) the left foot. It is recorded in the medieval poem *Gawain and the Green Knight*. **Kay-pawed** and **kay-fisted** are common northern dialect words for left-handed, both of which can be used to express clumsiness (as in the more standard **cack-handed**), and **kay-legged** seems, therefore, to mean 'having left-handed legs' with an implicit sense of clumsiness or ungainliness. This transfer of the senses associated with left-handedness may well have been influenced by the earlier **jay-legged**.

See KNOCK KNOCK, p. 122, *and also* JAY-LEGGED, KNAP-KNEED

keepie-back

savings (northern England; especially used in 'Pitmatic')

While **keepie-back** can mean money saved for a rainy day, it could also mean the money earned by miners for overtime, and which was kept hidden by miners for spending on beer and gambling. It was used particularly by the mineworkers in the local pits of Northumberland and Durham, whose dialect has emerged as something distinct from Geordie or Northumbrian thanks to the wonderful lexicon that emerged from the mining communities, known as 'Pitmatic'.

Kerr-handed

left-handed (Scotland)

The left-handed lexicon is a big one in dialect terms: most of the many synonyms for being a **southpaw** (a term from baseball referring to left-handed pitchers throwing with their arm facing the south side of the ballpark) are locally specific. Depending on where you are in the country, you can be **corrie-handed**, **Kerr-handed**,

kay-pawed, **cack-handed** and **caggy-handed**. Scotland probably tops the list as the most prolific source of left-handed words. Simon Elmes, while researching *Talking for Britain*, discovered that within a 14-mile radius in Scotland there are fourteen different variations for being left-handed. What is more extraordinary is that almost all seem to relate to the Kerr family from Ferniehirst Castle in the Scottish Borders.

Legend has it that the Laird of the castle, Andrew Kerr, was left-handed, an attribute he found extremely useful in battle, for it allowed him to surprise the enemy with the unexpected direction of his sword. Not only that, but Kerr employed only left-handed soldiers. The castle itself was built to maximise this advantage: whereas in most castles the staircases spiral clockwise, Ferniehirst has counter-clockwise ones, providing left-handed swordsmen with an advantage – the bends give a defender's left hand freedom to move over the open railing.

See also CUDDY-WIFTER, KAY-LEGGED

knap-kneed
knock-kneed (the North-West, East Anglia and Lincolnshire)

Knap is an Anglo-Saxon word meaning 'the crest of a hill', which later came to mean more generally 'a bump or protuberance' in some areas. **Knap-kneed** is most common in East Anglia and south Lincolnshire, but **knappy-kneed** is found in Cheshire and Derbyshire, and **knapper-kneed** is also recorded in Cheshire. In Devon and Somerset, the two 'n'-sounds are characteristically inverted in **knee-knapped**.

See KNOCK KNOCK, p. 122, *and also* JAY-LEGGED, KAY-LEGGED

Knock knock

If you have knees that knock together you will be known as **knock-kneed** across most of Britain, or something close to it. You may be **knocker-kneed** in Lancashire and Yorkshire and across the northern parts of Cheshire, Staffordshire and Lincolnshire, **knocky-kneed** to the north-west of that as far as Westmorland, and **knack-kneed** and **knacky-kneed** to the east of that. **Knack-kneed** can also be found in the South-West. **Knap** is used to replace **knock** in a number of places, especially East Anglia, while in the South-West, formations with **knap** get reversed so that **knee** comes first, as in the equally alliterative **knee-knapped**. **Knee-knocked** has also been recorded in Dorset, **knee-knabbed** in Devon, while **knacker-kneed** can be found in Yorkshire and **knuckle-kneed** in Suffolk. What is most striking is that these variations all preserve the jangly double 'n'-sound of **knock-kneed**.

There are some exceptions to the alliterative rule: **cock-kneed** (Lincolnshire), **crab-ankled** (Lincolnshire), **crooked-legged** (Yorkshire) and **hurked-up** (Warwickshire).

See also JAY-LEGGED, KAY-LEGGED, KNAP-KNEED

la (lah)

a term of affection (Liverpool)

> This term, frequently added to the end of a Scouse sentence, is
> regularly used to signify Liverpudlian heritage, as it is in the name of
> the 1980s rock band The La's, best known for their song 'There She
> Goes'. The apostrophe in their name is correct, **la** being a
> contraction of lad. Today la can be used to address either sex in
> much the same way as mate or love is used elsewhere in Britain.

laidly

hideous, repulsive (Scotland and Northumberland; now rare)

> A northern variant of **loathly** (basically equivalent in meaning to
> loathsome), **laidly** has been used in the north of England and in
> Scotland since the fourteenth century. The ranges of uses it shows
> cover physical repulsiveness ('His laidly legs and arms covered with
> sores'), offensiveness and hatefulness ('With laidlie language, loud
> and large'), and clumsiness or ungainliness ('A laidly flup, a clumsy
> and awkward fellow'). The word is now vanishingly rare, but many
> of its uses are mirrored in modern Scots by **minging**.

> *See* THE MIRROR CRACKED, p. 31, *and also* BUTTERS, DUFFY, FUSTY, MINGING,
> MUNTER, OBZOCKY, RANK, SKANK

laik

to play a game (Yorkshire)

If you are **laikin at taws up a ginnel** you are likely to be playing marbles up a Yorkshire alley. **Laik** derives from a Middle English word **laike**, which in turn derives from an Old Norse verb meaning 'to play'. **Laikins**, up north, are toys, while in Yorkshire **laiking** can also be taking a day off work.

Lark, not dissimilar, may indeed be one and the same word, since it has been suggested that it is no more than a Yorkshire pronunciation of lake, as heard by visiting jockeys, sportsmen and the like who frequented the county's hunts and horseraces. However there may equally likely be a link to the slightly earlier **skylark**, which, with its origins in the Royal Navy, must have referred to sailors scampering up and down the rigging of the nation's 'wooden walls' (or defence ships).

Lake is primarily found in Yorkshire, and literally means 'to exert oneself', 'to move quickly', 'leap, spring' and even 'to fight'. Also spelt **laik**, it has further uses including to play or to sport, with the amusements including the 'game' of romance, or, as previously noted, taking a day off work.

lampered

worn out, exhausted (Cornwall)

To be **lampered**, at least in Cornwall, is to be exhausted. Contrary to expectation it has nothing, even figuratively, to do with turning one's lights out. The origin lies abroad, in the Norwegian dialect word *lampa*, 'to walk with heavy steps', 'to beat or thrash', suggesting the dragging steps of a tired person who **lamps** or **lampers** – or clumps along. The **lamp** itself represents the style of walking, while a **lamper** is a tall heavy woman. Lampered milk, meanwhile, has coagulated.

See ALL PAGGERED AND POOTLED, p. 115, *and also* BLETHERED, BUSHWHA, DIRT DEEN, JIGGERED, MAGGLED, WABBIT

leer/leery

hungry (the South)

> From a thirteenth-century word meaning 'empty', **leer** and **leery** have been used since the nineteenth century in the South, east of Dorset, and in the South Midlands, to mean 'hungry'. The form **lear** is also common. The suffixed form leery becomes more common the further west you go, being recorded chiefly in Dorset and Somerset, but also in Devon and Cornwall where it comes second only to **thirl**. Like many words from the South-West, it is also recorded in Newfoundland in Canada.

> *See* LEERY FOR LUNCH?, p. 106, *and also* CLAMMED, CLEMT, HUNGERED, YAP

lerrups

rags; shreds (Cornwall)

> To **larrup** is to thrash violently (and is related to the equally aggressive to lace or to leather), often found in the context of the mythical but ever-popular Wild West. **Lerrups** are rags or shreds – with which some hapless varmint has been presumably larruped. A favourite Cornish expression, meanwhile, is to **scat t'lerrups**, meaning 'ruin beyond repair'.

> In a less melodramatic context, those same rags can also be scraps of butcher's meat, or simply the rags of tattered old clothes. Whether it is the same word or otherwise, a **lerrup** can also be defined as 'a lazy slovenly fellow' or, in the female context, 'a slut' or 'a trollop'. Perhaps the idea is that their morals are 'in tatters' too?

lish

active (of a child) (chiefly the North-West)

> **Lish** is probably a shortening of **lissom** with the final -s being changed to -sh (a fairly common linguistic phenomenon). It is recorded in Yorkshire from the eighteenth century with the meaning of 'agile' (and is also recorded in Scotland, especially in the

By the way

Alleyways are, like brooks and rivulets (*see* WATER WATER EVERWHERE, p. 170), exquisitely local places. They exist almost on the boundary between public and private space, dark, secluded, their existence rarely widely known. They represent local knowledge at its most local and most practical in terms of geography, and the words for them do the same linguistically. Where they differ from the brooks of the countryside is in being part of the urban landscape. From the **ginnels** and **snickets** of Yorkshire and Lancashire, to the **twitchels** of the East Midlands, and on to the **ennogs** and **jiggers** of Liverpool, these local alleyways are embedded in the culture of the industrial towns and cities of northern England, as short cuts, meeting places, escape routes. Even **alley** itself is first recorded in the early sixteenth century describing the narrow back streets of early modern London. An alleyway in this sense is perhaps best described as something that you duck down.

That is not to say, however, that the alleyway is only urban. There is a similar rural tradition of words describing narrow country lanes, often between hedgerows. The **loans** and **loanings** of northern England and Scotland are just two examples, as are the **lokes** of East Anglia.

And that's not all, for there is also a collection of other terms that all point to the importance of having a local term for those important byways of the village or town, where a lot of business (romantic, friendly and not so friendly) took place. They include **close** (Scotland and the North), **drift** (East Anglia), **drove** (East Anglia and South-West), **gully** (Lincolnshire and Berkshire), **jennel** (North-West), **jetty** and **mear** (Leicestershire), and **tenfoot and twitten** (Sussex).

See also ENNOG, ENTRY, GINNEL, JIGGER, LOAN, LOKE, SNICKET, TWITCHEL

form **leish**). The application to an active child is located chiefly in North Yorkshire, north Lancashire and Westmorland. Lissom is found in this sense in Wiltshire, Berkshire and Staffordshire.

See TEARDOWN TEARAWAYS, p. 179, *and also* UNEASY, WAKEN, WICK, YAP

loan

country lane (northern England)

Loan is a northern variant of lane. It has been used in Northumberland, Cumbria, Durham and North Yorkshire since the nineteenth century to refer to narrow country lanes enclosed by banks or hedges. In Scotland, the word typically refers not to rural alleyways but to a larger lane or street, such as the main road through a village. **Loaning** is an alternative in the north of England, although less common in Scotland.

See BY THE WAY, p. 126, *and also* ENNOG, ENTRY, GINNEL, JIGGER, LOKE, SNICKET, TWITCHEL

lobscouse

a sailor's dish consisting of meat stewed with vegetables and various other ingredients (Liverpool)

> 'So have up the anchor, let's get it away.
> It's a good grip, so heave, bullies, way-ay!
> Saltfish an' lobscouse for the next half year
> She's a Liverpool packet an' her Ol' man's the gear.'

So goes the sea-shanty 'Rio Grande'. Setting aside what looks like a very early example of the use of gear as an expression of approval, and as popularised by Liverpool's much-loved Fab Four, saltfish may be familiar, but **lobscouse** is a little less obvious. Lobscouse is in fact one of sea-going northern Europe's best-known dishes, known in Norway as *lapskaus*, in Sweden as *lapskojs* and in Denmark as *labskovs*. The Hamburg version consists of corned beef, gherkin, beetroot and potatoes with an egg on top, but there are many others, the basics being meat, vegetables and potatoes. A meatless version is known as **blind scouse**. The exact origin of the word is debatable, but one expert suggests a blend of **lob**, 'to bubble', and **lolly**, 'a broth'.

Most significantly though, the word, thanks to its maritime links, is the root of **Scouse** or **Scouser**, 'a Liverpudlian' (and the dialect they speak).

loke

country lane (East Anglia)

Loke has been consistently used in East Anglia since the eighteenth century at least, always referring to a country lane which is enclosed by banks or hedges, or which is sometimes private property. It derives from an Anglo-Saxon word meaning 'enclosed place'. Lokes resemble urban alleyways in often being short cuts or secretive cul-de-sacs. A translation of the Song of Solomon into Norfolk dialect made in the nineteenth century sings, 'In the lokes and causeys I'll seek him as my soul do love.'

See BY THE WAY, p. 126, *and also* ENNOG, ENTRY, GINNEL, JIGGER, LOAN, SNICKET, TWITCHEL

mackem

a native of Sunderland; a supporter of Sunderland Association Football Club (northern England)

The origin of **mackem** remains obscure, but there are many popular myths about it, which are worth the retelling.

One belief is that it was a term used by shipyard workers in the nineteenth century on the Tyne to describe those who lived in Wearside. The Geordies from Tyneside would take to be fitted the ships made in Sunderland, hence the phrase **mack'em and tack'em** ('make them and take them'). A centenary programme from the Sunderland Cricket and Rugby Football Club in 1973 carries the slogan 'We still tak'em and mak'em and you cannot whack'em.' Some also maintain that mackem is a reference to the Second World War, when the Wear was a major supplier of ships, giving birth to the phrase 'we mackem and they sink em'.

The term is not popular with everyone. Some see it as a label of insult, used particularly by Newcastle United fans when claiming superiority over Sunderland United. The two cities have a history of rivalry beyond the football pitch, dating back to the early stages of the Civil War when Newcastle became a Royalist city and Sunderland, partly influenced by its large contingent of Scottish traders, supported the Parliamentarians under Oliver Cromwell. Whatever its origin, mackem is likely to remain contentious. While some wear the term with pride, for others it is the ultimate put-down born of a rivalry that is centuries old.

made up

happy (Ireland and Liverpool)

> First recorded in Ireland around the end of the Second World War, **made up** made its way to Liverpool, the city often referred to as the unofficial capital of Ireland. From Liverpool it began to pass to more general use largely through the influence of TV. The *Oxford English Dictionary* cites an ITN interview with Ringo Starr on his wedding in 1965, in which he tells us that John and George were made up, only to add a quick explanation that 'they're happy'. No such explanation would be needed now, as the word has spread out from Liverpool and gained a good foothold in general use.

maggled

tired out, exhausted (South Midlands)

> **Maggled** is to be found in a string of counties from Worcestershire right through Gloucestershire and Oxfordshire to Berkshire. The verb **maggle** is probably a variant of **mangle** and is recorded with the meanings of 'maul, maim, lacerate' from the early fifteenth century. **Magged** has been recorded in Bedfordshire in the same sense. **Razzored** (from razored), from Derbyshire, is probably a parallel formation, the idea being of falling to bits through exhaustion.
>
> *See* ALL PAGGERED AND POOTLED, p. 115, *and also* BLETHERED, BUSHWHA, DIRT DEEN, JIGGERED, LAMPERED, WABBIT

mai

grandmother (London and UK-wide)

> This Hindi word, meaning 'mother' or 'mother-in-law', provides an excellent example of a common and longstanding linguistic phenomenon whereby the word for mother is used more generally as a respectful title for older female relatives, especially a grandmother. In this case the shift has happened not

in Indian English per se, but in the English of the Indian communities in the Caribbean, in Trinidad and Guyana, where the title is applied both to grandmothers and to older women in general. The word is also now a familiar one in the language of Hinglish: the rich mixture of Hindi and English which is growing rapidly in Britain.

See OH MAI, p. 148, *and* GANNY, GRAMMER, NAIN

malleted
drunk (Liverpool and Birkenhead)

If you are **malleted**, you are well and truly drunk, and would probably feel as though hit by a mallet. The term sits alongside **mangled**, **mashed** and **massacred** in Scouse-speak (and beyond), as one of hundreds of euphemisms for 'flying three sheets to the wind' (there's another).

See LIQUID LUNCHES, p. 70, *and also* BLOOTERED, DRUCKEN, DRUFFEN, FLUTHERED, PISHED, PUGGLED, SKIMMISHED, STOCIOUS

mammy
mother (the North)

Like **mam**, **mammy** means 'mother', and the *English Dialect Dictionary*'s first examples for both lie in the Shetland Islands. But mammy has gained less positive overtones through its use for the stereotyped black retainer, straight out of *Gone With the Wind*, tending her white charges on a slave-run American plantation. A nineteenth-century lexicographer called it a 'term of tenderness' and linked it to Romany **mami**, 'a grandmother', but a century later the black writer Zora Neale Hurston dismissed it as 'a term of insult'.

manshon

bread roll (chiefly northern England and Cornwall)

Like **barm cake**, the **manshon** is found mainly in the north of England, and also in the South-West (especially Cornwall in this case). It's unlikely that this means there is some historic, bread-based link between those areas, but rather that they are two of the principal dialect areas outside the South-East, which has historically been the focus of standard English. It is a small loaf, shaped like a bun, but can also describe a muffin or a hot cake.

Manshon appears in the *English Dialect Dictionary* in many spoken forms, including **manchent**, **manchun**, **manshen**, **manshun**, **manshut** and **mansion**. Its most likely background lies in the Norman French word *manchette*, which literally meant a 'double-cuff or oversleeve' (in modern French it means a 'headline'), but which was also used to describe a ring-shaped cake of bread. There is, however, an alternative theory, based not on the look of the loaf, but on the quality of flour it required. Such flour would be sifted through some kind of a narrow bag, which in French was a *manche*, literally a sleeve or strainer used for the filtering of that high-grade flour to deliver 'wheat bread of the finest quality'.

By the end of the fifteenth century, a manshon was already being used to refer to fine bread rolls (Edward IV is recorded as eating them for breakfast), making it the only word to refer specifically to a bread roll before roll did.

See OUR DAILY BREAD, p. 49, *and also* BAP, BARM CAKE, BUTTY, COB, NUBBIES, STOTTY

mardy

sulky, sullen; spoilt (northern England, particularly Yorkshire, and the Midlands)

If a child is **mardy**, he or she is over-indulged, or simply badly behaved. In other words they are spoilt, and it is very likely that mardy is in fact a simple variation of marred. To **mard** a child was to spoil them by indulgence, and a mardy can describe such a child as well as their undesirable behaviour. These attributes are not restricted to children, though, and an adult can be just as mardy – or indeed be a **mardy-arse**: in other words whining, sulky and moody.

Mardy as a noun first appeared in the 1870s, and as an adjective a few decades later in the early years of the twentieth century. It has remained in favour since, although it became even more popular thanks to the 2006 release of the song 'Mardy Bum' by the Brit Award-winning band the Arctic Monkeys, featuring the lines:

> 'Well now then Mardy Bum
> Oh I'm in trouble again, aren't I
> I thought as much
> Cause you turned over there
> Pulling that silent disappointment face
> The one that I can't bear.'

On a similar theme, **mardy-arse** denotes a spoilt brat.

If marred is the generally accepted root of mardy, there are other suggestions too, including one that links mard to French *merde*, 'excrement'. Both Derbyshire and Lincolnshire possess the noun **mardo**, used of excrement when talking to very small children. If this theory is correct, then mardy-bum and mardy-arse, usually used to tease some hapless youngster, carry the strongly implied suggestion that the person in question is still in nappies.

See THE MARDY BLUES, p. 134, *and also* COB ON, TATCHY

The mardy blues

Words describing a bad-tempered, fractious person who is prone to sulking once abounded in local dialect, from the standard moody and sulky to the old East Anglian word **pensy**. Historically, there is a remarkable concentration in the area of the eight counties of the Industrial Revolution (Yorkshire, Lancashire, Cheshire, Staffordshire, Warwickshire, Derbyshire, Nottinghamshire and Leicestershire), including **humpy**, **kysty**, **maungy**, **nattered**, **nazzy**, **neppered** and **nousty**. Alas, most of these words appear to have dwindled over the course of the twentieth century. It is still the case, however, that the most distinctive current regionalisms for moody arise in this region.

See also COB ON, MARDY, TATCHY

marra

friend (Northumberland)

In Northumbrian pits (where the language of 'Pitmatic' was born), you may hear **marra**, short for marrow and originally denoting 'one of a pair'. Its etymology, sadly, is uncertain, although it may derive from Old English **mearu** or **maro**, meaning 'a companion', or from Old Icelandic *magr*, which meant 'friendly'.

See also BLOOD, BREDREN, BUTTY, CATERCOUSIN, CHUCK, CLICK, CREW, HOMIE, MUCKER, SORRY

mash

to brew tea (the North and Midlands)

It may not be the image that springs to mind as the boiling water enters the pot and gently infuses the tea leaves (for the word, like the action, long pre-dates the tea bag) but, according to the *English Dialect Dictionary*, the word **mash**, for adding hot water to tea, originally meant 'to beat violently', as of course in mashed potatoes.

The explanation for the tea usage lies in brewing, for the term also refers to the process of infusing malt in hot water so that the sugars dissolve, hence the wonderful-sounding **mash-mundle** or **mash-mungle**, an implement used to stir the malt and water mixture. The ultimate roots of mash may lie in a variety of Scandinavian terms, all of which stress the same brewing context, and may even go back to the German word *meischen*, meaning 'to tread grapes'.

Mash was first recorded in relation to tea in the mid-nineteenth century, and became the standard term for brewing tea throughout the North and Midlands, up as far as North Yorkshire, in distinction from the more general **brew** in the South. It may be significant that the area it covers includes most of England's principal brewing areas.

See KETTLE'S ON, p. 185, *and also* BIRLE, EMPT, HELL, MASK, SCALD, SOAK, TEEM, WET

mask
to brew tea (Scotland and northern England)

Mask is simply a variant of **mash**, found in the very northern part of England (Cumbria, Northumberland, Durham, the far north of Yorkshire) and in Scotland. The extension of the term from brewing to tea, however, seems to have occurred slightly earlier than with mash. The *Oxford English Dictionary* records a first date of 1799.

See KETTLE'S ON, p. 185, *and also* BIRLE, EMPT, HELL, MASH, SCALD, SOAK, TEEM, WET

May gosling
April Fool (Lancashire, Cumbria and Yorkshire, now rare)

Not strictly an April Fool, **May gosling** was a parallel tradition held on 1 May throughout the region for which **April noddy** is recorded. It is mentioned in the eighteenth century, and the celebrated collectors of children's rhymes, Iona and Peter Opie, found the custom alive and well among schoolchildren in the 1950s. **Gosling** is recorded as meaning 'a foolish, inexperienced person' in Scotland in the early nineteenth century.

See A PINCH AND A PUNCH, p. 3, *and also* APRIL GAWBY, APRIL GOWK, APRIL NODDY, FOOL GOWK, HUNTIGOWK

How to talk like ... **the Welsh**

Well, look-you, it depends which Welsh. Now do you mean *North* Walian, or *South* Walian, isn't it? And that's the question, of course guaranteed to raise hackles in the land of the daffodil and the leek. As are likewise the stereotyped 'look-you' inversion and 'isn't it' tag that have all the hallmarks of the mocking imitator. The Welsh have had a hard time of it from the English for centuries – the Welsh language was persecuted and in centuries past schoolchildren heard speaking it were forced to wear a wooden collar, known colloquially as the 'Welsh-Not', to deter them from doing so again.

And there's not a lot of love lost either, it seems, between the north and south of this long country, divided by mountains and deep valleys, with only Offa's Dyke keeping the English at bay. A South Walian, living in Anglesey, complains, 'People regularly say "Pakistani, are you?" because my accent is still so South Walian.' The north, with the greatest concentration of native Welsh speakers, tends to feel threatened by people from the south, whose English constantly runs the risk of overwhelming the old language.

Naturally, too, north and south have very different social traditions. South Wales was for generations the great manufacturing and industrial heart of the country with its 'vaalleys' studded with coal mines, now gone, and the vast steelworks of Port Talbot, today shrinking fast. North Wales, apart from slate mining, has a largely rural and farming tradition. And the accents of the country tend to reflect these very different cultural shapes.

So in the south the short vowel 'a', as in *valleys*, is lengthened and *back*, *lamb*, *accent* and so on all sound more like 'baak', 'laam' and 'aaksent'. These lengthened sounds work in tandem with the tune of South Walian English, to produce what's almost always referred to as a sing-song accent, but which more accurately is a combination of lengthened vowels, heavy syllabic stress and many elided syllables (even between words) to produce marked rhythms and an almost melodic rise and fall. 'He juss TAD ti CHEInge is AAKsent, an' issAD' ('He just had to change his accent and it's sad') said one South Walian of her son who'd been bullied by classmates for speaking with a strong accent. Note how the 't' of *just* has elided with *had* ('juss tad') and again *it's sad* is slurred together becoming 'issad'. And among the vowels, the 'ay' long vowel has a dash of 'ee' in it: *change* is 'cheinge' and under this regime, the country itself is pronounced as 'Weels'.

The open 'o' vowel of *know*, *toe* and *go* is regularly pronounced in South Wales as an 'aw' sound; so one stubs one's 'taw' and 'gaws' to the doctor to have her examine it; meanwhile *I don't know* becomes something like 'Adawnaw'.

There's a tendency to pronounce the *-ing* at the end of present participles and gerunds as 'en' so *saying* and *going* become 'sayen' and 'goen'. And (classic lampoon fodder this) the 'h' in word-primary position (*here*, *hearing*) doesn't simply disappear as so often in British dialects (notably in the South-West), but transforms itself into a 'y' sound. *Here* is 'yer' (leading to the mocking over-use by imitators of expressions like 'down by yer'), and 'yerring' is *hearing*: 'AdinYER' is the response of someone who failed to catch what they'd been asked. Just to complicate matters, one's hearing apparatus sounds here identical, leading to such indignant phrases as 'Cant yer? Yuse yer yers, boyo!'

As with Gaelic speakers in Scotland, those whose native tongue is the distantly related Celtic language of Welsh have a much softer, more sibilant sound to the English they speak, which produces a sort of lisping effect when using words like *pity* which becomes 'pitsi'. Alongside this is the tendency of these first-language Welsh speakers to de-voice consonants where in standard English they would be voiced, or hard. So 'g' is de-voiced to 'k' and 'd' to 't'. Lamented one elderly North Walian about the threats to her native Welsh language: 'I like them to keep the Welsh language koin'. I think itss a pitsi to lets it ko.'

As in the south, there is a rise and fall in the tune of North Walian, but it's a more staccato sound, with less of the flowing up-and-down rhythm of southern speakers. The north is also a 'rhotic' area, so the 'r' in a phrase like 'awuR (our) grandparents' is audible, while in South Wales, there is no r-sounding.

While the long north–south border with England is quite marked in terms of accent, that around the eastern extremity of North Wales in Flint, on the Welsh side of the Mersey estuary, shows considerable overlap. Here the Welsh takes on a decided tinge of Merseyside with trailing word-ends and added sibilance. As one local said, 'I've been taken for a Scouser: very often the people say, "You're proper Scouse, Man! You're not Welsh."'

Duw (God) man! It's **pickin'** (beginning) to rain. **Twti down** (crouch) and fetch the **daps** (plimsolls) in. My **gwennie** (trendy young woman)'s just gone up the **gwli** (alley) to buy some **loshins** (sweets) and forgotten to **keep the dishes** (put them away), **isn't it** [standard tag-word]. Her **nain** (grandmother) will be furious as she's a **tidy** (decent) soul. **Yachy da!** (goodbye!).

SIMON ELMES

mazy

giddy, dizzy (the North-West)

> **Mazy** is a fairly straightforward image of confusion ('like a maze') found in English since the beginning of the sixteenth century. By the middle of the eighteenth, it had become most prominently a Lancashire word. Unsurprisingly, however, it is also recorded in neighbouring counties, Cheshire, West Yorkshire and north-west Derbyshire, as well as in nearby Staffordshire.
>
> *See* GOING SWIMMINGLY, *p. 204, and also* REEZIE, SWIMY

meat

food; nourishment (in pockets across the UK including Shetland and Scotland)

> **Meat** is food. It was quite literally that because, prior to the fourteenth century when meat began referring specifically to the flesh of animals that had been killed and which had been subjected to some form of cooking – in contrast to the bones and other inedible parts – meat was defined as any kind of food, both for people and, indeed, as fodder for animals. In other words it meant solid food generically, as opposed to drink, as well as an article of food or a dish of food. It could also be a meal or, more elaborately, a feast, and as such could signify the principal meal of the day. So the phrase **at meat and meal** means 'at the table' or 'during a meal', and **after** or **before meat** refers to the meal, not a course. To **go to meat** was in days gone by to sit down to eat, even if the food was fish.
>
> The root of meat lies in a variety of Celtic languages, but beyond that its root is a little hazy. The best guess is some kind of link to Latin *madere*, 'to be wet, succulent or fat'.

Meg-many-feet

a centipede (Ireland, Northern England and Scotland)

This alliterative term for a child's favourite insect has many local alternatives, including **Meggy-Mony-Legs** in Scotland and **Meggy-Monyfeet** in Northumberland. A spider's web, meanwhile, is known in the same parts as **Meggie-lickie-spinnie**.

Meg's diversions

boisterous, noisy antics (Wiltshire)

Also known as **Meg's Delight** (though why they should belong only to Meg is a mystery), **Meg's Diversions** was a term first recorded in the army in the early 1800s, where it described frivolous fun to be had when off-duty.

messages

shopping (Scotland, Ireland and in Caribbean English)

A **message** began life, in the 1300s, as the business of carrying or delivering a communication; a mission. From there it took on the general sense of going out and running an errand, with no transmission of a message being required. And so **doing the messages** became doing the shopping, where it has settled to this day.

midden

dung heap (Yorkshire)

A **midden** has been a dung heap since the 1400s, and it survives in Yorkshire to this day. In fact the word was around even before that in Old English, and can be found in the ninth-century *Lindisfarne Gospels*. It lies behind such place names as Northumberland's Blacmyddingmore (now Blackmiddingmoor). There are numerous midden compounds, including the wonderfully alliterative **midden mavis**, a woman who collects rags and rubbish (restricted to Scotland

and now, sadly, largely obsolete). Elsewhere, midden is used across Britain in archaeological contexts, where it denotes a prehistoric refuse heap marking an ancient settlement, consisting chiefly of shells and bones and often also discarded artefacts. The word is, fittingly, a mixture of two Scandinavian terms meaning 'muck' and 'dung'.

minging

ugly; rubbish (UK-wide and particularly Scotland)

For a dialect word that began life meaning 'a mixture', **minging** has done spectacularly well, having become one of the most popular of the put-downs currently on offer. Literally it means 'stinking', but the focus of its use may be just as much emotionally unappealing as actually smelly. The word comes from **ming**, which is Scottish for stink (and, in the past, excrement), and thus the **minger** or **minga** is the literal equivalent of the rather old-fashioned English **stinker**. While the Scots verb has been around for many years, **minger**, **minging** and the rest came south in the 1970s, and have become increasingly widely used. Rab C. Nesbitt captures most of the range of meanings pretty succinctly: 'Thae weans are the fruit of my loins. Awright my loins might be minging and the fruit a bit bruised aboot the extremities, but I brought thae boys into this world.'

As well as a derogative, minging can also mean 'drunk'. The suggestion of a nasty smell, of course, is always there.

See THE MIRROR CRACKED, p. 31, *and also* BUTTERS, DUFFY, FUSTY, LAIDLY, MUNTER, OBZOCKY, RANK, SKANK

mitch

to play truant (the South-West, Wales and Ireland)

Mitching comes from an Anglo-Norman term for hiding or concealing oneself, and first took on the meaning of 'absenting oneself from authority' in the late 1500s. In 1672, the author and physician Henry Stubbe was writing about 'truant children, who forsook their school, to go mitching after black-berries'. Francis

Grose, meanwhile, has it in his *Provincial Glossary* of 1796 that **mitch** meant 'to slink, slouch, prowl about, idle about', and hence a **mitchin** was a sly, skulking, mischievous boy and a **micher** or **michard** an idler, loafer and a truant. But mitch is certainly the earliest established synonym for playing truant; by the nineteenth century, its use was distinctively found in the South-West and South Wales, and later Ireland. Father Ted, for example, said that he 'mitched off to see a Dana concert'. A variant in Wales is **mitsian**. Interestingly, Francis Grose also defined **mooching** as playing truant, with the specific aim on the part of the children of picking blackberries. There is in fact very likely to be a close link in the origins of mooching and mitching.

See BUNKING AND PLUNKING, p. 192, *and also* BUNK OFF, DOG, NICK OFF, PLAY HOOKEY, PLUNK, SAG, SKIDGE, SKIVE, TWAG, WAG

mither

to worry, fret, make a fuss or moan (northern England and the Midlands)

The root of **mither** is probably a development of **moither** or **moider**, meaning 'to confuse, perplex or bewilder', as well as 'to worry, fatigue or bother'. To be **moithered** is to be overcome or stupid with heat or drink, while the adjective **moithering** can also mean delirious or bewildered. The origin of all terms, for all their emphatic force, is unknown. Perhaps the most likely candidate is **maythering**, a word that describes talking like an imbecile, although the Irish word **modartha**, meaning 'dark', 'musky' or 'morose', is another possibility.

mizzle

light rain, drizzle (chiefly the North and Midlands)

Mizzle is a word of Dutch and north German origin that was first recorded in English in the middle of the fifteenth century. For centuries, it seemed to have no regional affiliation and was used by numerous canonical authors, including Spenser, Swift and Austen. Over the past two centuries, however, the word has become mostly restricted to the North and Midlands and also to the South-West. Interestingly, the word also remains common in the American South. It may come from a Dutch word *mysel*, but whatever its origins its alliterative association with drizzle is unmistakable, as is its wonderful sound.

See DON'T TALK DRIZZLE, p. 10, *and also* BANGE, HADDER, SMIRR

moldwarp

the European mole (Scotland and northern England)

A compound of the Germanic words mould and warp, and literally meaning 'earth-thrower', **moldwarp** is a name used in the northern UK for the much maligned mole. Cited in the *Oxford English Dictionary* as far back as 1325, this term is most commonly used in Scotland. In 1595, Spenser wrote in *Colin Clouts Come Home Againe*, 'They . . . drownded lie in pleasures wastefull well, In which like Moldwarps nousling still they lurke.'

mollycrush

to hit or whack (Wales, the Midlands and northern England)

Mollycrush or **mullicrush** means, depending on the context, 'to beat to a jelly', 'to pulverise', 'to bruise' and, in figurative uses, 'to hector or domineer'. Although the molly part might be seen as linking to the use of that word for a girl, and the stereotyping of females as weaklings, the greater likelihood is that the verb derives from the word **mull**, describing something that has been reduced to minuscule particles.

See A TWANK AND A WALLOP, p. 15, *and also* BENSIL, THRAPE, TWANK

mooch

See MITCH

moonraker

a native of Wiltshire (south-west England)

The Swiss lexicographer Francis Grose, best remembered for his *Classical Dictionary of the Vulgar Tongue*, tells in another important work, his *Provincial Glossary*, the legend of Wiltshire 'moon-rakers', 'rusticks who, seeing the figure of the moon in the pond, tried to rake it out'. Today's moonrakers would dispute that strongly, and counter with the alternative story that the men were in fact raking a pond for kegs of smuggled brandy. When they were caught, they managed to fool the revenue men by feigning madness, pretending to be raking the water in order to find the moon.

More prosaically, but rather more plausibly perhaps, a **moonraker** is also a high sail, set about the sky sail: so high, in fact, that it appears to be touching the moon. Few, however, would prefer this over the romance of the smugglers and their passion for brandy.

morgs

money (Lincolnshire; now obsolete)

Although there seems to be only a single recorded instance, **morgs** is the best example of a genuinely regional piece of slang meaning 'money'. The isolated example comes from the complaint of a Lincolnshire man at the end of the nineteenth century: 'He has plenty of morgs. He owes me morgs.' Its etymology is not known.

See MONEY TALKS – OR DOES IT?, p. 144, *and also* ACKERS, GELT, REVITS, SPONDULICKS

Money talks – or does it?

Most European languages have a vast and vivid array of informal and slang words for money, and English accepts second place to no language in the vastness and vividness with which it denotes **cash**, **ackers**, **dosh**, **wallop**, **spondulicks**, **bread**, **cabbage**, and so on. Although all of these words except cash (from the sixteenth century) are pretty recent, they merely replaced another list of words from an earlier era, like **blunt**, **crap**, **gingerbread** or **rhino**. In spite of, or maybe even because of, this host of informal terms, there is alas no great history of regionally specific words that just mean 'money'. Where regional terms for money have been recorded, they are normally used to describe particular sorts of money that have some local significance. For example, **kaird turner** was once used in Scotland to denote small coins made from base metals by tinkers, and in Northumberland and Cumbria **ball-money** was money demanded at the church gates from the bridegroom and other men in a wedding party as a contribution towards parish funds (originally to buy a football for the parish!).

Beyond that, the predominant regional words for money are very often some of the older slang words from centuries ago, simply because so many of them arose within the London area as the code of criminals, tinkers, and other people living on the margins of society.

See also ACKERS, GELT, MORGS, REVITS, SPONDULICKS

mort

a woman; a harlot (Cumberland)

> The official origin of **mort**, meaning 'a woman', is unknown.
> However, the fairly frequent linking of women to fish through the
> ages (for coarsely stereotypical reasons) makes it at least possible
> that the word comes from mort, a 'young salmon'. However it may
> also be linked to one of two Welsh words: **modryb**, 'a matron', or
> **morwyn**, 'a virgin'. In criminal slang, where mort was once one of

the best-known terms for a girl, you could find such compounds as **mort dell**, an unmarried woman or virgin girl who accompanies an itinerant villain or beggar, and **mort wap-apace**, an experienced prostitute or sexually active woman. In this case she was characterised by **wap**, which meant 'to have sex', and **apace**, 'speedily'.

The lexicon of terms for women is full of words such as mort which have both 'virgin' or 'harlot' as their potential meanings. Housewife and hussy both originally meant the same thing – 'a mistress of the house' – before going in their two respective, and extreme, directions.

mucker

friend (UK-wide but particularly Northern Ireland and the Black Country)

In Northern Ireland and the Black Country, the word **mucker** has undergone many shifts of register, from negative to positive. Its earliest meanings were literal ones: first recorded in the thirteenth century, it referred to a cleaner of stables who removed dung, and could also denote a person who prepared soil for planting. In the early 1800s it started to be used to describe someone who bungled things and who was therefore incompetent. This sense of contempt was strengthened when mucker took on, in nineteenth-century America, the sense of 'a troublesome or rowdy person'. It also, in American university slang, denoted a **townie**.

It wasn't until the mid-1900s that mucker began to take on positive connotations, first within British military circles and then more widely. It denoted 'a close companion or friend', with whom you regularly socialised or 'mucked in' – which originally meant to share rations. It is often used as a form of address – the *OED*'s first quotation is 'what's the griff [news] mucker?', from a military novel set in the Second World War.

See also BLOOD, BREDREN, BUTTY, CATERCOUSIN, CHUCK, CLICK, CREW, HOMIE, MARRA, SORRY

mullock

a mess (Yorkshire)

Mullock, 'a mess' in Yorkshire, comes from the word **mull**, meaning 'something that has been reduced to small particles' such as dust, ashes, mould or rubbish. The word is linked to those in a variety of northern European languages such as Dutch *mul*, meaning 'mould or dust', the German *Müll*, 'rubbish', and Old Icelandic *moli*, a 'crumb'. The first recorded use of *mullock* seems to be in 1199, where it appears as the surname of one Jordanus Mulloc, who might well have been a contemporary dustman.

Other than its regional use, mullock can mean 'a worthless, foolish individual' and, in the Antipodean goldfields, is a rock which does not contain gold, or alternatively the refuse from which gold has already been extracted. The phrase **to poke mullock (at)** means 'to ridicule or make fun of someone', as in Donald Stuart's novel *I Think I'll Live*, set in the prisoner of war camps in Java, 'You're no Mister bloody Australia y'self . . . so don't poke mullock at anyone for being a bit skinny.'

munter

an ugly man or (usually) woman (London and UK-wide)

Munt, in Suffolk, means 'an inferior kind of fire-clay'. Maybe this use links to **mount**, used in Ireland to refer to a slatternly girl or woman (or a girl who is perceived as such). It is definitely a variant on the word **munter**, described in one dictionary as an ugly girl who is 'one step up from a minger'.

See THE MIRROR CRACKED, p. 31, *and also* BUTTERS, DUFFY, FUSTY, LAIDLY, MINGING, OBZOCKY, RANK, SKANK

nailbourn

an intermittent stream (Kent)

One of the few words for a specific type of stream, **nailbourn** is recorded in Kent as far back as the fifteenth century, and it has stayed in Kent ever since. The -bourn part of the word is the southern form of the northern **burn**, but the origin of the nail- isn't clear. One suggestion is that nail- is in fact ail- , and refers to a stream which is a source of disease. The n- is then explained as a misanalysis of an ailbourn as a nailbourn (this is a common linguistic phenomenon known as metanalysis; apron, for example, was originally **napron**). We may, unfortunately, never know for sure.

See WATER WATER EVERYWHERE, PX, *and also* BECK, BURN, PRILL, RINDLE, SIKE, STELL

nain/nin

grandmother (North Wales/Liverpool)

From the Welsh word for grandmother, **nain** is found in all parts of Wales. It also gives rise to the Liverpool equivalent **nin**, recorded from at least the late 1950s and once so distinctive that it has been said every true Scouser has three relations – 'Me Mar, Me Nin, an me Anti-Mury'. Nain itself is recorded in Welsh English from the early 1950s and is particularly common in the parts of North Wales where Welsh is spoken.

See OH MAI, p. 148, *and also* GANNY, GRAMMER, MAI

Oh mai

The most striking, but ultimately not really surprising, thing about words meaning 'grandmother' is how closely they parallel the words for 'grandfather'. For **grammer**, see **granfer**; for **grammy**, see **granfy**. With the Welsh **nain**, compare **taid**. Even stranger formations frequently match up. The Manx **grandmayer** has its cognate in **grandayer**, and the unusual **baba** is related to **papa** ('b' and 'p' are the same consonant but said respectively with the voice and with the breath only), being recorded in Berkshire in the very region where 'p-' words for grandfather are most common.

There are, however, two important exceptions to this rule. One is gran, which is the most widespread and commonly used term of all. There is no obvious reason why gran should be used of a female grandparent rather than a male, but there is the powerful motive to avoid ambiguity dictating that it must only be used for one of them. So, in the battle for space that that implies, the women have won hands down. The other exception is provided by words like nan, nanna and nanny. These probably derive from the female forenames Anne and Agnes, and were originally used with the sense 'nursemaid'. They have all become fairly common across the country from the South-East to Manchester and Liverpool. Nana, for example, is used in the TV comedy *The Royle Family*.

There are a handful of other variants too, no less affectionate. They include **baba** (Berkshire), **grammy** (Lincolnshire), **grandmam** (North-West), **grandmayer** (Isle of Man), **grandmum** (East Anglia), **grandy** (Scotland), **mai** (London and now moving throughout the UK), **mam-gu** (South Wales), **nanna** (South, especially the South-East), **nannies** (Berkshire), **nanny** (Norfolk, Shropshire) and **nin** (Liverpool).

See also GANNY, GRAMMER, MAI, NAIN/NIN

nazzard

an insignificant or mean person (northern England)

An extract in the *Oxford English Dictionary* from a 1963 collection of Yorkshire yarns entitled *Aald Taales* includes the wonderful line: 'Didta ivver see sic a wurm itten **nazzard** i' thi life?' Look at the word **nazzardly** (or **nizzardly**) and you'll find an equally evocative line, from a full three centuries earlier: 'Such a nazzardly Pigwiggin, A little Hang-strings in a Biggin.' (A Pigwiggin, or **pigwidgeon**, was a fairy or elf, and a **biggin** was a night-cap.) Both demonstrate the sheer onomatopoeic verve of the word nazzard, which has ensured its survival today and its use by young as well as old.

neb

to nose around (the Midlands and Northumberland)

To **have a neb** means literally to 'have a nose', which in Northumberland has the figurative meaning of 'having a stare or peek at someone'. As far back as Old English, **neb** has denoted the bill or beak of a bird, and similar terms can be found in a wide range of northern European languages, among them the West Frisian *nebbe*, Norwegian *nev* and Swedish *naef*. At the same time, Shetland Scots offers **nev**: a beak, a point, or the handle of an oar. But there's more. Add the prefix s- and you can find the Dutch *sneb* and *snab* and the Old Frisian *snabba*, all of which mean 'a mouth'. It is through this link that you see a direct connection with a horse's snaffle, a form of bridle-cum-bit.

ned

a young person in trendy clothes and flashy jewellery (Scotland)

The Glaswegian **ned** was symbolic of the sharp end of urban working-class youth culture long before the subculture associated with designer sportswear and bling developed. It emerged in the early twentieth century to describe a good-for-nothing or low-life, and soon developed a stronger strain implying that the person was a thug or petty criminal. Recently, however, it has become increasingly employed as the Scottish synonym for a **chav**. This development has come hand in hand with the adjective **neddy**, often used to describe the distinctive clothing associated with the subculture. The word probably derives from the informal form of the name Edward.

See THE CHAVS AND THE CHAV-NOTS, p. 43, *and also* CHARVER, CHAV, JANNER, KAPPA SLAPPER, PIKEY, SCALLY, TROBO

neighbour

to gossip (Yorkshire)

Neighbouring, the friendly association with fellow members of your village or community, was a common phenomenon in the nineteenth century, and it didn't always involve the spreading and exchange of gossip. But clearly it usually did, which was why the word quickly developed the specific subsense 'to gossip'. The verb was formerly recorded in most parts of Scotland and England, but in the Survey of English in the 1950s, the specific sense was collected only in Yorkshire. The verb **to house** (and the noun **houser**) are parallel formations in Cornwall.

See ALL THE LOCAL GOSSIP, p. 34, *and also* CANK, CANT, CHAMRAG, CLISH-MA-CLAVER, COOSE, JAFFOCK, JANGLE, PROSS, TALE-PYET

nesh

susceptible to cold; damp and chilly (Scotland and the South-West)

Softness and delicacy are probably not what tends to cross the mind as you battle home through an icy storm, but language has no time for meteorology, and **nesh**, which means 'damp, moist, wet and chilly', in places from Scotland through to the south coast, is linked to a number of European terms that mean just that. For instance there is the regional Dutch word *nesch*, meaning 'soft' (of eggs) and, way back in 1550, 'damp, sodden or foolish'. Similarly there is the Gothic *hnasqus* which meant 'soft or tender'. For all these, the word's ultimate origin remains, sadly, obscure – and so the leap from soft to shivering is a mystery.

See BLOWING HOT AND COLD – MOSTLY COLD, p. 152, *and also* NITHERED, SHRAMMED, TATERS

netty

lavatory (the North-East)

Writing with a reticence that you might not expect to come from the supposedly gritty North-East, J. T. Brockett put it this way in his *Glossary of North Country Words* of 1825: '**Netty**, a certain place that will not bear a written explanation, but which is depicted to the very life in a tail-piece in the first edition of Bewick's "Land Birds" (1797), p. 285.' For those who lack the time to check, the netty, sometimes **neddy**, is of course a public lavatory, as it is called in Newcastle and environs. Its etymology is popularly supposed to be an abbreviation of the synonymous Italian *gabbinetti*, 'toilets', but unfortunately not a shred of evidence exists to make the international link. An alternative is a corruption of the seventeenth- and eighteenth-century slang **necessary** (house), meaning 'a privy'. One last suggestion links it to the French verb *nettoyer*, 'to clean'. None of these are proven; yet the netty is still going strong across the North-East.

nick off

to avoid or slip away (UK-wide)

The verb **nick** has meant 'to avoid', 'to slip away', or 'to leave on the spur of the moment' since the nineteenth century, and probably began its life in Australian English. It clearly then returned to Britain and was picked up by schoolchildren as code for bunking off school. These senses strongly suggest a link with **in the nick of time**. The northern term to **nick off**, meaning to 'go off' or 'away' surreptitiously or hurriedly, appeared around 1900, although – like all slang – its spoken use almost certainly pre-dates printed records.

See BUNKING AND PLUNKING, p. 192, *and also* BUNK OFF, DOG, MITCH, PLAY HOOKEY, PLUNK, SAG, SKIDGE, SKIVE, TWAG, WAG

Blowing hot and cold – mostly cold

The British Isles are an archipelago in the North Atlantic. Go up to the north of Scotland, to Aberdeen, say, and you are further north than Moscow. Being cold literally comes with the territory. And so it is that bad weather, in dialect terms, seems to accrue more words than good weather. Many more, in fact. Whether you are chilly, lightly drizzled upon or up to your neck in mud, you can bet on the fact that somewhere around your corner is a bit of linguistic local colour waiting for you.

In common use we have words for when it really is emphatically cold, so cold that you might freeze (freezing) or even die (perishing), and for when it's cold, but not *that* cold, when it's just chilly. But there are a plethora of ways of expressing the fact that it is cold, which convey just how cold it is by describing more vividly the effects on the speaker, such as **Baltic** and **bitter** (terms which are now UK-wide), **nithered** (northern England and Scotland), **shrammed** and **mopy** (the South and South-West) and the evocative **hunchy** (Cambridgeshire). These words are often derived from dialect verbs meaning 'to shrivel' or 'to make numb'.

More recently a number of equally colourful slang words used to describe cold weather have emerged and passed into general use, such as **brass monkey weather** (which was first used in the United States), **parky** (which seemed to emerge among well-heeled huntsmen, game shooters and anglers in late nineteenth-century England), and **taters** (which is Cockney rhyming slang). According to a list drawn up by an American linguist called Morris Swadesh in the 1950s, the word for cold is one of the hundred words least likely to change in a language (the list is used by linguists to help measure how related two or more languages are), and it's probably because so standard a word seems so basic, so ordinary, so dull and obvious that people feel the need to come up with alternatives which are a bit more vibrantly expressive.

See also NESH, NITHERED, SHRAMMED, TATERS

nithered

cold (northern England and Scotland)

This enduring term literally means 'shrivelled or stunted by the cold'. It comes from an Anglo-Saxon word meaning 'to oppress or humble'. The word survived only in the north of England and Scotland, and by the end of the seventeenth century it had taken on the association with cold that it retains today (it can also be used of hunger). Such eminent northerners as the former MP Austin Mitchell, and the darts commentator Sid Waddell, define the word in their *Teach Thissen Tyke*: '**Nithered**, very cold. A condition found on the kind of day that affects brass monkeys adversely.' An equivalent further south is **shrammed**.

See BLOWING HOT AND COLD – BUT MOSTLY COLD, p. 152, *and also* NESH, SHRAMMED, TATERS

no-mark

a nobody; a failure (Liverpool and now UK-wide)

No-mark, meaning 'a good-for-nothing' (and as an adjective used to describe something or someone worthless), started off life in Liverpool: the first recorded use is in an episode of *Brookside*, written by Phil Redmond, in 1982. The image is of something that lacks any mark or stamp of approval or origin, and is a direct descendant of America's much earlier **no-account** or **no-count** (literally 'one who is of no account', i.e. estimation or esteem), which are a good century older – no-count appears for the first time in 1852 in Harriet Beecher Stowe's anti-slavery story *Uncle Tom's Cabin*. For all its late start in life, however, no-mark looks set to stay.

nubbies

plain yeast buns (Cornwall and the South-West)

The name **nubbies** probably comes from **nub** or **nubbock**, 'a lump'. As you might guess, the buns are about as simple as their linguistic background: and delicious with it.

See OUR DAILY BREAD, p. 49, and *also* BAP, BARM CAKE, BUTTY, COB, MANSHON, STOTTY

nuddle

to walk with one's head stooped (Suffolk, East Anglia and Northamptonshire)

To **nud**, in Cheshire and in Shetland, is what animals do when they butt or nudge their heads while feeding – in other words they nuzzle. This is the probable root of **nuddle**, which a human might do when elderly or when simply lost in thought.

nugget

someone of limited intelligence (Liverpool)

The *English Dialect Dictionary* defines **nugget** as 'a lump', and it is presumably as a figurative lump that the word is used in Liverpool to describe a fool. Like dense, which can mean 'thick' both as to physique and as to brain-power, so too can nugget, for it also means 'a small, compact or stocky animal or person'. The word is probably linked with the words **nudge** or **knudge**, which have been terms for a lump or a thick-set person as far north as Dumfriesshire and as far south as Devon.

nummit

a light meal (Devon and Wales)

Nummit is the name for a light meal, generally taken in the middle of the day by farmhands while working in the fields. Believed to be a variation of **noonmeat**, referring to a meal eaten around noon, records of the term date back to the late eighteenth century, especially in the West Country and in South Wales. A **dew-bit** was a small meal or portion of food eaten early in the morning, before a proper breakfast. The form **nammet** is also common.

See CLOCKING UP YOUR CROUSTS, *p. 214, and also* BAG, BAIT, CLOCKING, JACKBIT, SNAP, TOMMY

obzocky

ugly (Caribbean communities across the UK)

Like **duffy**, **obzocky** is a Caribbean word which has passed from Britain's Caribbean (in this case Trinidadian) community into wider British use. Richard Allsopp's *Dictionary of Caribbean English Usage* gives it the following definition: '(of furniture, clothes, colours, etc.) Misshapen, ill-fitting, very odd-looking . . . (of person) ungainly and badly dressed (especially of women) fat and wearing conspicuously ill-chosen colours . . .' Also like duffy, obzocky means 'ugly' and derives from a West African language (there is a possible root in the Yoruba word *obo*, meaning 'a monkey' and also 'to break wind', thus implying a connection with the Guyanan term **monkey-fart** which means 'absolute nonsense').

Apart from that, duffy and obzocky are fundamentally different, and they demonstrate the division between older and newer words for ugly. The two words arise from the two largest Caribbean communities in the country, and in different cities. Whereas duffy is Jamaican and Liverpudlian, obzocky is taken from Trinidadian Creole in London (in the Caribbean itself, it is found in a number of the islands of the Lesser Antilles). Whereas duffy is concerned with sexual attractiveness, obzocky is not concerned with that at all. It is closer in meaning to awkward or ungainly, and has a sense of things looking just not quite right. People can be obzocky, but so can buildings, cars, animals – almost anything, in fact.

See THE MIRROR CRACKED, p. 31, *and also* BUTTERS, DUFFY, FUSTY, LAIDLY, MINGING, MUNTER, RANK, SKANK

offcomeduns

an outsider (Yorkshire)

> *See* WOOLLYBACK

oggy

a pasty or pie (Cornwall)

No holiday to the South-West is complete, of course, without a packed lunch including a pasty, or **oggy**. Originally a Cornish oggy was a pasty half-filled with meat and vegetables and half with fruit such as apples. The term is probably an alteration of the Cornish word **hoggan**, meaning a 'pastry or pie', perhaps linked with a much older Welsh term **chwiogen**, a delicious-sounding muffin or simnel-cake. The first citation of oggies in the *OED* comes from the 1948 *Dictionary of Forces' Slang*, but the word is still going strong. The *Daily Telegraph* reported fairly recently that 'the battle could begin between the Big Mac and the West Country oggie . . . The pasty has long been a staple for seafarers in Plymouth.' It is said that each ship in harbour receives a daily delivery of hot oggies.

The chant 'Oggy! Oggy! Oggy!', to which the traditional response is 'Oi! Oi! Oi!', often heard at sporting events and also the chorus of a Cornish folk song, is most likely also related to the pasty. One popular theory is that the wives of tin-miners and pasty-sellers supposedly shouted 'Oggy! Oggy! Oggy!' to announce the arrival of hot food; the response from any hungry miner or labourer would be 'Oi! Oi! Oi!'.

> *See also* CLANGER, CROGGY, HOGGAN

oorie

gloomy, cheerless; out of sorts (Scotland and Ireland)

For the Scots and the Irish **oorie** fits many situations in which the overall feeling is one of gloom or low spirits. Sadly, its origin is unknown, although the *Scottish National Dictionary* speculates that there may be a connection with the verb **owl**, which means 'being muddle-headed even while appearing wise like the owl'.

ornery

ordinary (UK-wide but particularly Devon and the South-West)

It is hard to believe that so, dare one say, ordinary a word as
ornery might once have been regarded as so 'shocking' a term
that it should 'never pass the lips of anyone'. However, this was so,
according to the late Allan Walker Read, a lexicologist who found it
as one of nineteenth-century America's coarse synonyms for the
word lewd. On the whole, however, ornery has been anything but
sexual, with meanings including 'of poor quality', 'commonplace',
'coarse', 'unpleasant', 'illiterate', 'mean' and 'cantankerous'. Its
derivative **orneriness** describes feeling tired or vaguely unwell.

oxter

armpit (Scotland, Ireland, the Isle of Man and north of England)

Nowadays, the term **armpit** for that hollow under our arm goes
almost unchallenged in southern England and in the North-East,
while **armhole** enjoys currency in the North-West and much of the
East Midlands and Norfolk, extending sporadically as far south as
Buckinghamshire and Essex. But, oblivious to both pits and holes,
Scotland and the very north of England have had **oxter** as their
standard term since the fifteenth century, and the word is also
found in Ireland and on the Isle of Man.

Oxter is first recorded in the Borders in the early fifteenth century
and is of Germanic, and perhaps specifically Scandinavian, origin.
By the end of the sixteenth century, it can found as standard in
Scots texts of all kinds – literary, historical, legal, scientific. Eminent
Scottish or Irish writers who used the word include Swift, Sir Walter
Scott, James Joyce and James Kelman.

A verb **to oxter** also developed with a number of meanings,
such as 'to support under the arms', 'to put one's arm around' and
'to carry under the arms'. It is first recorded in Burns's poem 'Meg
o' the Mill', in which a drunken priest is 'oxter'd' to the altar to
perform a ceremony. The following example from 2000 suggests

that the nature of society may have changed more over the past two centuries than the nature of the word: 'She had to be oxtered out of the city-centre-style bar while the night was extremely young.'

pace egg

a decorated egg at Easter (northern England)

The egg is a pagan symbol of the renewal of life – an apparently
inert object from which new life emerges. It was rapidly adopted by
early Christian tradition as a symbol of Christ's resurrection and,
hence, of Easter. Easter eggs, however, only became chocolate in
the twentieth century. Before that a much older tradition held.
Hard-boiled eggs were painted in bright colours and then rolled
down a hill or slope before being recovered and eaten. The painting
of eggs in this way remains a common Eastertide occupation of
schoolchildren, especially in the United States, but the tradition of
rolling is now much rarer. So common was it once in northern areas
of England that the day the rolling took place (usually Easter
Monday, but also Easter Sunday or even the Tuesday) was known
as **bowl-egged Sunday**, **roll-egg day** or **bowling-egg day**. It is in
the North as well that the only common regional alternative to the
standard term is recorded – **pace egg**.

Pace is a Scottish and northern English variant of **Pasch**,
meaning Passover or Easter, which is itself derived from the Latin
word *pascha* (with the same meanings). Pasch is pronounced
with a 'k' at the end and the dropping of the 'k' is typical of
Scotland and the very north of England. Pace egg is recorded in
the south of Scotland, Northumberland, Cumbria, Yorkshire and
Lancashire.

As with Easter eggs in the rest of England, pace eggs were traditionally rolled down a hill or slope on Easter Sunday or Easter Monday. Pace egg also came to be a term for Easter itself with Easter Sunday being known as **pace egg day**. **Pace-egging**, meanwhile, described the egg-rolling tradition and the performance of traditional Easter mummers' plays. These plays were known as **pace egg plays** and were common throughout the region. In fact, many local pace egg plays have been revived in recent decades.

pank

to pant (the South and South-West)

Recorded throughout the South-West and as far east as Berkshire and Hampshire, **pank** is the most common regional alternative to pant, but it is also the most difficult to explain. The tempting assumption that it is simply a version of pant is probably wrong, because that alternation of 't' and 'k' would be unique, and is therefore doubtful. Perhaps it represents not a variant but a deliberate alteration of pant to increase its imitation of the sound we make when we breathe fast and loud.

See A PILE OF PANTS, p. 209, *and also* THOCK, TIFT

pasty-footed

splay-footed (Lancashire)

The meaning here seems to be 'with feet spread out like paste'. The word is first used in 1607 by Thomas Dekker and John Webster in their play *Northward Hoe*, where it is a general term of abuse: 'You **pasty-footed** Rascalls.' It is possible that the recent Lancastrian use retains some negative connotations too, because at the end of the nineteenth century, a **pasty-foot** is recorded in West Yorkshire, referring to a ghost, or a tramp.

See NO MEAN FEET, p. 62, *and also* DEW-FOOTED

pax

a word used by children to declare truce in a game (the South-East)

Pax is Latin for 'peace'. The word has literally hundreds of equivalents in children's games up and down the country. In northern England you might hear **barley** or **kings** (said while crossing your fingers). In Ipswich, if you don't want to be kissed during a game of kiss-chase, you say **exsie**, while in London, as well as pax, you could say **faynights.** In Scotland you can choose from an entire lexicon, including **barrels**, **bees**, **tibs**, **dibs**, **dubbies**, **peas**, **pearls**, **parleys** and **paxman**. Other colourful alternatives from the South include **creamos**, **creamy olivers**, **scribs**, **scrunch**, **ollyoxalls**, **double queenie** and **fingers**.

peelie-wallie

pale, sickly (Scotland)

Peelie-wallie, or **peely-wally**, means 'pale, sickly or ill-looking'. It may have arisen because of its sound, which imitates a feeble whine, and there is in fact a dialect word **pee-wee** which means 'whining' or 'small'.

The second part of the term, wallie or wally, is probably related to the word **wallydrag**, which according to the *English Dialect Dictionary* describes 'a feeble, ill-grown person or animal, or a worthless, slovenly person, especially a woman'. One example from the *OED* from 1879 begins with 'yon bit pernicketty wallydraggle!' While wallydrag dates back to the sixteenth century, though, peelie-wallie itself didn't begin to appear until the 1830s. It remains an evocative term in Scottish dialect for feeling under the weather.

How to talk like ... a Brummie

Well, forget trying to make people love your accent, for a start. The speech of Birmingham, the Black Country and the West Midlands in general has repeatedly over many years come out bottom or next to bottom in polls of Britain's favourite accents, usually alongside Scouse.

Just what it is that people find to object to is actually hard to determine. It's an urban form of speech, and along with the accents of London, Bristol and other big conurbations, Brummie can be a bit flat. And it's a rather nasal accent, of course, which can sound as though the speaker's suffering with a heavy cold.

But I guess above all what marks out the accent of the Birmingham area most of all is its upwardly inflected intonation pattern and flattened vowel sounds, most of which seem to have played musical chairs in the mouth. So 'i' shifts to 'oi' (*right* pronounced as 'roight'), 'a' (*may*) becomes 'my' and 'o' (*low*) moves over to 'aow' (as in standard *mouth*). Long 'ee' goes south towards long 'a' such that *treat* becomes 'trayt'.

Sometimes this great Birmingham vowel shift can prove confusing, as Professor Clive Upton of Leeds University, the country's foremost expert in regional English and himself a Brummie, has observed. With the standard 'oi' sound becoming something akin to a triphthongised 'aoi' sort of noise, 'If you hear someone say that someone's got a "naoice vaoice" it'll be hard to say whether they've got a nice *voice* or a nice *vice*,' he says.

So when encountering a female chum, your matey Brummie, using the local dialect term 'bab' for girl might well say 'All right, bab?' except that this will emerge something like 'Oroit, bab?' And if you're feeling a bit negative and *don't want* to do something, in Birmingham this shifts along from 'don't' to 'daynt'. And sometimes these mobile Midlands vowels can make comprehension doubly tricky for the non-habitué of New Street, as she's informed that her male friend has just been to the new Bullring shopping centre to buy some 'stroids'. Stroids, she wonders? And then the Perry Bar penny drops and she performs the necessary double translation: 'stroids' are *strides* and strides are (as in parts of northern England) trousers.

And that connection with northern English is not fortuitous: the Birmingham 'u' belongs firmly to the same family as its Yorkshire and Lancastrian cousins, and makes it not so 'toof ter'oonderstand, this Broomie' when you lend a northern ear to the sound. Likewise that useful little intervening 'r' that's a familiar feature to lovers of Lanky dialect appearing where no 'r' is ever printed turns up here from Edgbaston to Erdington as in 'gerroff' for *get off* and 'gerraway' for that expression of surprise, *get away*.

So the sound of Birmingham belongs to itself, with plenty of nods to its neighbours to the north, but it also very much doesn't display any of the rubicund 'r' sounds that we associate with the cider orchards of the South-West, which also spread up into the rhotic areas of the south-west Midlands from the Gloucestershire borders. So a Brummie, remembering the rougher tougher time of a working-class childhood in the city, will say it was 'a very haad loife' (*hard life*), unlike his cousin from Devon who'd remember that 'life wuz 'aRRd'. Another sound that's never on the page but which creeps into the way words are pronounced in the city is the intrusive 'k', such that the place is often heard talked of by locals as 'Birmingkham'.

So Brum talk is characterful, urban, distinctive. It does amazing things with vowels in so radical a way that only an Ulsterman would find the changes unsurprising, and yet along with Liverpudlian and Belfast the speech of England's second city rarely attracts praise, but often mockery and even shame. As one Brummie admitted to a dialect researcher: 'I watch the tallay, an oi see soombody interviewing a Birmingham person on the tallay and oi think, God, that's awful!'

A passenger gets off the train at New Street in Birmingham and is immediately enveloped in the talk: '**Worroh**!' says one local in greeting; '**Oorroit**!' replies another. The taxi driver, waiting in line for fares, complains that it's **parky** (chilly) this morning, though his passenger's thinking to herself he's a bit of a **morkins** (idiot) for being grumpy (or **mardy**, as she puts it). But despite the uncomfortable atmosphere, both cabbie and fare are happy to bid farewell to each other with an exchange of '**Tarrah**' and '**Trarabit**' (see you later). 'But he had **a fayce loik a bostid boot**' she complains to her **mom** at **hum** (home) later, 'he were that ugly! Spent the whole journey **canting** (talking), and waving his fat hands about' (or **donnies**, she calls them). Her mum, fed up with her childish attitude, ends the exchange with a curt 'Stop being such a **tittybabby**.'

SIMON ELMES

pikelet

a crumpet (northern England and the Midlands)

> The **pikelet**, the crumpet by many alternative geographical names, is variously defined, at least in the UK, as 'a thin kind of crumpet', a type of 'small round teacake made of fine flour', and 'a muffin'. In Australia, whence it presumably travelled with the early immigrants, it is a type of drop scone. On any account it is a tasty abbreviation of the Welsh **bara pyglyd**, 'pitchy bread', which may be a reference to its colour.

pikey

a term of insult (originally the Isle of Sheppey but now UK-wide)

> The word turnpike began life meaning just that: a spiked barrier fixed across a road as a defence against sudden attack, especially one from men on horseback – who would have been carrying pikes. Gradually it became used to describe any barrier, including those of water, but by the seventeenth century was best known as the abbreviation of turnpike road, a road that had a barrier at which a toll must be paid before one could pass through it.
>
> Many people rode and walked the turnpike, among them the Gypsies, a name itself based on Egyptian, a mistaken reference to the country from which they had supposedly come (the actual one being India). Gypsies had a poor and often unfounded reputation. Their nicknames reflected it, among them **pikey-man**, shortened to **pikey** and first used by locals on the Isle of Sheppey to describe the nomadic, allegedly disruptive strangers who turned up for the annual harvest. Pikey has more recently surfaced as one of the many synonyms for the regrettable term **chav**, the current term of choice for Britain's social underclass.

See THE CHAVS AND THE CHAV-NOTS, p. 43, *and also* CHARVER, CHAV, JANNER, KAPPA SLAPPER, NED, SCALLY, TROBO

pill

a tidal creek (south-west England and Pembrokeshire)

> A number of place names on both the English and Welsh banks of
> the Severn estuary include the word **pill**, such as Magor Pill in
> Monmouthshire, and Black Pill near Swansea. The word derives
> from the Old English **pyll**, meaning 'a pool or tidal creek'.

pished

drunk, intoxicated (Scotland and Northern Ireland)

> A variant of pissed, **pished** is recorded continuously in Scots for all
> the various senses of piss since the renownedly earthy poet of the
> very early sixteenth century, William Dunbar (the first writer to use
> the f-word). It is also found in the fifteenth century in the north of
> England. For example, while in general English a dandelion is
> sometimes called a **pissabed**, in nineteenth-century Scotland, it
> could be a **pish-the-bed** (in both cases because of the well-known
> diuretic properties of the plant). The sense 'drunk, intoxicated' is
> recorded in the twentieth century, following on from the same
> extension of pissed in England in the late nineteenth, and is now in
> ordinary informal use. The novelist Irvine Welsh is an especially
> prolific user of the word, both in its literal sense: 'Pished yir keks,
> Franco? Rents asks him, pointing at a wet patch oan the faded blue
> denim' (*Trainspotting*), and its metaphorical: 'We were pished
> senseless before we knew it' (*Glue*).
>
> *See* LIQUID LUNCHES, p. 70, *and also* BLOOTERED, DRUCKEN, DRUFFEN,
> FLUTHERED, MALLETED, PUGGLED, SKIMMISHED, STOCIOUS

play hookey

to play truant (originally New England, now across the UK)

> Now well known in England, this synonym for playing truant
> originated at the end of the nineteenth century as a regional
> American use from Pennsylvania. It was a development on an
> earlier phrase **to hook Jack**, used in New England and especially
> Massachusetts, with **Jack** simply being used as a generic term for

someone who might **hook school** – a later version to be found in Maryland and Virginia. The verb **hook** means 'to steal'; first recorded in the seventeenth century, it was principally an American word by the nineteenth. This group of **hook** phrases represents, therefore, an American parallel to British formations arising from steal words, like **nick** and **mitch** and, indeed, to **steal** away.

See BUNKING AND PLUNKING, p. 192, *and also* BUNK OFF, DOG, MITCH, NICK OFF, PLUNK, SAG, SKIDGE, SKIVE, TWAG, WAG

plodge
to wade through water or mud (Northumberland and Scotland)

Think **plodge**, and you think of the juvenile delights of rubber boots immersed in sucking mud, and further of the wonderful Northumberland phrase **plodging in the clarts**, 'to paddle in the mud'. In addition comes **plodger**, perhaps even more pleasing a word, which means 'a paddler or wader' (in water as well as mud) and **plodgy**, a description of deep snow that has yet to be marked by the imprint any foot.

See MUD, MUD, GLORIOUS MUD, p. 196, *and also* CLART, SLOB, SLUB, SLUCH

plunk
to play truant (Scotland)

Plunk is first recorded in mid-western Scotland and has been common ever since, mainly in the southern half of the country. Nowadays, **to plunk it** and especially **to plunk school** are the usual expressions. One Scottish journalist in 1997 recalled that 'Me and my mates didn't plunk school except to go and see Rangers playing Moscow Dynamo.'

See BUNKING AND PLUNKING, p. 192, *and also* BUNK OFF, DOG, MITCH, NICK OFF, PLAY HOOKEY, SAG, SKIDGE, SKIVE, TWAG, WAG

pollywog

tadpole (the South-East)

Pollywog is a synonym for tadpole, and makes its first lexicographical appearance in 1440, when the *Promptuarium Parvulorum* (a terrifyingly sober-sounding dictionary aimed at schools) offers 'Polwygle, wyrme'. The term exists throughout the British Isles, and is also to be found in North America. Spellings are various: **porwygle**, **poddywig**, **periowiggle** and **pollywriggle** among them. As far as can be established, the polly part comes from the fifteenth-century word **poll** which referred to the head of a person or animal, while wog seems to be linked to **woggle**, itself a variant of **waggle** (i.e. of the tadpole's tail).

prill

stream, rivulet (south-west Midlands and south-east Wales)

First recorded in the works of the Herefordshire writer John Davies, in the early seventeenth century, **prill** is a word that has always been associated with the counties either side of the southern half of the Welsh border. It is probably derived from **pirl**, an older word with the same meaning.

See WATER WATER EVERYWHERE, p. 170, *and also* BECK, BURN, NAILBOURN, RINDLE, SIKE, STELL

Water water everywhere

Streams and rivulets are an integral part of the countryside and have for centuries been vital to local communities as sources of water, boundary markers, and so on. Part of their usefulness is precisely their localness, their separateness from the rivers which acted as the main thoroughfares of rural life. As one nineteenth-century writer said, 'Each gorge and valley has its beck.' He, William Black, was Glaswegian, so he might also have said **burn**. If he had been from the Welsh valleys, he may well have said **prill**. If he had been from the Derbyshire Dales, perhaps **rindle**. And so on.

The words to be found are strikingly old. Many are of Anglo-Saxon origin and very few are not established by 1700. To the modern, urbanised eye, they also *look* old: **eas**, **pinnocks**, **holls** and **sikes** are the kind of thing we expect to find in the countryside, or perhaps more accurately in a nineteenth-century novel set in the countryside, such as William Black's *The Strange Adventures of a Phaeton*, quoted above.

The usefulness of these words, however, continues for the people who actually live among them. Take a winding path around the country's byways and you will find: **brook** (South), **burn** (Scotland and northern England), **creek**, **trickle** and **dyke** (Yorkshire, Derbyshire, Oxfordshire, Norfolk, Lincolnshire, Nottinghamshire and Kent), **riverlet** (Kent), **ditch** (Norfolk, Essex, Berkshire and Hertfordshire), **canal**, **lake** and **prill** (Wales and the Welsh marches in Monmouthshire), **beck** (North), **dingle** (Herefordshire), **drill** (Kent), **drain** (Norfolk and Lincolnshire), **sike** (Durham, Cumbria and Yorkshire), **stell** (Durham), **rindle** (Staffordshire, Derbyshire and Cheshire), **ea** (Lincolnshire), **nailbourn** (Kent), **gill** and **gote** (Yorkshire) and **holl** (Norfolk).

See also BECK, BURN, NAILBOURN, PRILL, RINDLE, SIKE, STELL

pross

to gossip (Durham)

Pross, yet another term for empty chitchat, with its adjective **prossy**, 'talkative', and the phrase **hold pross**, 'to have a gossip or chat', is no more than a dialect version of standard English's **prose**. Prose has been through various meanings through the ages, usually relating to technical aspects of writing, but it has settled down today to mean simply 'spoken or (usually) written language that is not subjected to any form of poetic rules'. To prose as a verb can be found regularly in the sort of early twentieth-century public school tales where it is synonymous with **jaw**, and it means 'to sermonise or to preach'. It is paradoxical, perhaps, that the underlying essence of prose has always been simplicity, clarity, the state of being matter-of-fact, while gossipy **pross**, on the whole, prefers the supposed matters to the actual facts.

See ALL THE LOCAL GOSSIP, p. 34, *and also* CANK, CANT, CHAMRAG, CLISH-MA-CLAVER, COOSE, JAFFOCK, JANGLE, NEIGHBOUR, TALE-PYET

puckle

an evil spirit or demon; a small amount (Scotland and the Midlands)

What links such place names as Puxton, Worcestershire and Pucklechurch in Gloucestershire and Shakespeare's *Midsummer Night's Dream*? It is the word **puck**, meaning primarily 'a malevolent spirit or demon', a 'bugbear' or 'bogey', and used as the name of the mischievous fairy in Shakespeare's play. **Puckle** is simply a variation of puck and means the very same thing. As for the village names, we are probably looking at the diminutive, still in Glaswegian use, puckle, meaning small. Pucklechurch is self-evident, but Puxton was originally Puclancyrce: again picking up on the 'small church' idea. Puck itself seems to be linked to a variety of Scandinavian words all meaning a wicked spirit, a goblin or even the devil. In a weaker sense, it can also simply mean 'a mischief-maker'. It is this same Puck that is to be found in the title of Rudyard Kipling's much-loved collection of children's stories *Puck of Pook's Hill* (1906).

puggled

crazy; crazy-drunk (Scotland)

A variant of **poggled**, the word **puggled** is based on the Hindi noun *pagal*, which means a 'madman' or 'idiot' and which was absorbed into English in the 1820s. A century later, both poggled and puggled were taken up in the Army as slang terms for crazy. The development of the sense of 'drunk', as in 'mad-drunk', was perhaps inevitable. They continue to be used particularly in Scotland.

The Anglo-Indian resonance of the word, and its origin in *pagal*, is evident in the final page of the Rudyard Kipling story 'Baa Baa Black Sheep': when the children have been reunited with their mother one of them says, 'Mother's never angry ... She'd just say "you're a little pagal"'. Meanwhile, the *Oxford English Dictionary* includes a quote from Brian Aldiss's humorous novel of military life in the Far East during the Second World War: 'A woman in this bloody dump? You're going puggle, Page, that's your trouble! Too much tropical sun.'

See LIQUID LUNCHES, p. 70, *and also* BLOOTERED, DRUCKEN, DRUFFEN, FLUTHERED, MALLETED, PISHED, SKIMMISHED, STOCIOUS

pumps

soft shoes (the Midlands, Yorkshire and the North-West)

Pumps have been shoes since the sixteenth century, far longer than any other word now used to describe gym shoes. They have not, of course, been gym shoes for that long! The word has been used to describe a variety of close-fitting, slip-on, low-heeled shoe: from slippers, to acrobats' shoes, to dancing shoes, and then, in the twentieth century, to school gym shoes. In this last use **pumps** comes a close second after plimsolls, and is standard throughout the Midlands, Yorkshire and the North-West.

See ANYONE FOR SANNIES? p. 99, *and also* DAPS, GUTTIES, SANNIES

pussyvanting

interfering, meddling (the West Country)

The adjective and noun **pussyvanting** is defined by the *OED* as 'an ineffectual activity or pointless bustle' (movement, that is, not the garment). It has more recently, and particularly in Cornwall and Devon, gained the added meaning of 'following someone around (usually of the opposite sex) in an irritating manner'. Its origins are not entirely clear: certainly there seems to be a play on **gallivanting**, meaning 'to gad about in a showy fashion', usually to amuse or entice the opposite sex. But why pussy? The cat's infinite capacity for wrapping itself round a person's legs is one suggestion. Alternatively **puss** and **pussy** have long since meant 'a hare' in dialect, and so perhaps the suggestion is of the hare's darting, zig-zag movements under pursuit. Natural history aside, it's also worth noting the *English Dialect Dictionary*'s account of what may or may not be a folk etymology, based on the arrival in the seventeenth-century West Country of **poursuivants**: crown agents who went around the country assessing those entitled to bear arms. Their interference would certainly not always be welcome.

q

quare

many, a great deal (Ireland)

'Tis quair things I have been seeing!' declared a letter written from Ulster in 1805, but there was nothing odd about the correspondent's experiences: he'd just had a good many of them. Whatever may have happened to **queer** (or as seen here in its regional spelling and pronunciation, **quare**) in the centuries that have followed, for those who choose it on the other side of the Irish Sea, the word is regularly used to refer to a large number, or as an intensifier. And so P. W. Joyce, in his guide *English as We Speak It in Ireland* (1910), refers to a day that was both 'quare and hot', encouraging him to get out there and enjoy it. Such a use of **queer**, which after all is almost invariably seen as a negative (originally by criminal beggars for whom it was the opposite of **rum**, meaning 'good or excellent'), leads to what otherwise might seem rather odd descriptions: 'She's a quare nice old lady.'

quilt

a wimp; a fool (Liverpool)

The link between **quilt**, a synonym for counterpane or duvet, and a Liverpudlian term meaning someone foolish, is presumably a pun: both are in their own way 'soft'. But it might be worth bearing in mind the *English Dialect Dictionary*'s definition of the noun as a 'pimple, a boil, or a blister', and of the verb as 'to beat up'. The meanings of the noun, then, tend to give the idea of softness, while the verb makes the victim so.

See DON'T BE DAFT, p. 89, *and also* ADDLE-HEADED, BARMY, DAFT, FOND, GORMLESS, SOFT

quobbled

(of hands) wrinkled, shrivelled (Wiltshire)

A hundred years or so ago, if a woman's hands had been immersed too long in the washtub, they were said to be **quobbled**, at least in the South-West. The word nicely fills the linguistic gap for the state of hands which, nowadays, have simply spent too long in the bath.

radgy

angry; bad-tempered (the North-East)

Radge is just a form of the word rage, and it is one which betrays its origins in the Scottish Borders. The earliest example in the *Oxford English Dictionary* is from the English side, Cumberland, in the mid-nineteenth century, although from later in the same century it had become much more common in Scots, and is still found there as well as in the North-East today.

Radgy is a distinctive word in contemporary Scots literature, to be found for example in the works of Irvine Welsh, Ian Rankin and many others. The alternative form **radgie** is also found in Scotland, but was also earlier recorded in the East Midlands, suggesting that it originally was indeed a Midlands word.

ram-stam

impulsive, impetuous, headstrong (northern England and Scotland)

As they say north of the border, 'These ranstamphis prickmadandies . . . brag and blaw sae muckle anent themsels.' Indeed they do, and **ram-stam**, whether of a **prickmadandy** ('a braggart or blowhard') or anyone else, means 'headlong', 'precipitous' or 'impetuous'. It also, perhaps predictably, refers to the strongest form of homebrewed beer. And the tongue-twisting **ramstamphis** means 'rough, blunt, unceremonious or noisy'.

The *Oxford English Dictionary*'s first evidence for ram-stam is from a poem by Robert Burns in 1786. In 1818 Sir Walter Scott wrote, in *Rob Roy*, 'The least we'll get, if we gang ramstam in on them, will be a broken head.' The origin is elusive, but the prefix ram is generally an intensifier (in such wonderful words as, for example, **ramfeezled**, meaning 'confused or muddled'), while **stam** means 'to walk with a quick, heavy tread', and so with purpose. The Cornish take on ram-stam is arguably even better: **ram-bang**, meaning 'headlong'.

rammel
rubbish of any kind (northern England and Scotland)

In Derbyshire **rammel** means 'worthless rubbish', while in North Staffordshire it denotes 'a mongrel dog'. In both cases, its extended meaning is of something unwanted and thrown away. Its origin, possibly, is in Old French *ramaille*, 'branches that have been cut from the tree', although there is no provable link and it may well be that this **rammel** is quite another word. Other dialectal meanings include 'loose, sandy, stony, hard or barren soil'. A **rammel cundy** is a drain filled with loose stones and as an adjective used of an animal **rammel** means 'big-boned' or 'scraggy', and, of a person, 'rather rough'. In Nottinghamshire it is possible to hear the powerful and dismissive threesome **piffle**, **rammel** and **twaddle**.

rank
ugly; inferior (now UK-wide but originally London)

Rank has meant second-rate, inferior or foul-smelling since the late seventeenth century. It is derived from the standard English term rank, meaning 'rotten' (usually of meat), 'rancid' or 'strong-smelling'. It is likely to be an import from Caribbean English, where it is primarily used as a pejorative, and a particularly severe one at that. The root, of course, remains the same: 'smelly'.

See THE MIRROR CRACKED, p. 31, *and also* BUTTERS, DUFFY, FUSTY, LAIDLY, MINGING, MUNTER, OBZOCKY, SKANK

Teardown tearaways: the active child

As any parent knows, an active child is a mixed blessing. At least linguistically there is a wealth of terms to describe this double-edged sword.

Active is found in all regions of the country, as is the similarly standard lively. The most common local alternative is **wick**, which can be found throughout most of the North. All of these are fairly positive in meaning, suggesting that the child is full of energy. **Lish, lissom, brave, fresh, frim, frisky** and **spry**, all accord with active, lively and wick. But others, like **bothersome, mischiefful, riving** and **wiggy-arsed** suggest that the adults' energy levels are not up to those of the children. Adjectival phrases are a feature of this group of words, again with distinctions of tone and register. **On the go** is common, especially in the East Midlands and the East Riding of Yorkshire, while equivalent, but less positive, phrases like **on the wander** and **on the fidget** are also recorded.

And so across the country you can still find: **bothersome** (Isle of Man), **brave** (Dorset), **fidgety** (all of England except Northumbria), **fresh** (Northumberland), **frim** (Leicestershire), **frisky** (Northumberland), **hardy** (Ireland and Newfoundland), **lissom** (Berkshire, Wiltshire, Staffordshire), **litty** (Somerset and Dorset), **mischiefful** (Essex, Wiltshire), **mischievous** (Leicestershire, Somerset and Norfolk), **pert** (central southern England), **quick** (Staffordshire), **riving** (Yorkshire), **sprack** (South-West, especially Wiltshire and Somerset), **spry** (Dorset), **upstrigolous** (Somerset), **wiggy-arsed** (Wiltshire); **(full of) ganning on** (Northumberland), **full of vim** (London), **on the fidget, on the rouk, on the wander** (Yorkshire); as a noun, meaning 'an active child': **chraddle-head** (Cornwall), **rake** (Berkshire) and finally **little lubber, rummager** and **tear-down** (Lincolnshire).

Quite a handful.

See also LISH, SKOPADIDDLE UNEASY, WAKEN, WICK, YAP

reen

an open ditch or water course (the South-West)

> Low-lying areas of England and Wales have often been drained
> artificially, and the man-made drainage channels are known as
> **reens**. The term is used widely in a number of counties, although it
> has a number of different spellings, including **rean**, **rhyne** and
> **rhine**. The idea for all is that of running water, hence the French
> term *rhume* for a cold, and, of course, the river Rhine.

reezie

giddy, light-headed (south of Scotland; now rare)

> At the beginning of the nineteenth century, James Hogg, a farmer
> and poet from Ettrick in south-east Scotland, followed his fellow
> poet from rural Ayrshire in the South-West, Robert Burns, into
> Edinburgh literary society. In 1815, another poet of the vogue for
> dialect poetry that Burns started, James Ruickbie, wrote of Hogg,
> 'Lang about Ettrick may ye toddle, And clew a poet's reezy noddle.'
> **Clew** means 'scratch', **noddle** 'the back of the head' and **reezy**,
> 'giddy', was one of the local words captured by this poetic
> movement. By the mid-twentieth century, it was rare and restricted
> to the Selkirk area.

> *See* GOING SWIMMINGLY, p. 204, *and also* MAZY, SWIMY

revits

money (Yorkshire; now rare)

This is probably a variant of **rivets**, which is first recorded as a slang term for money in the London underworld of the mid-nineteenth century. Referring mainly to coins, it is an extended use of rivet in its usual meaning of a 'short bolt for fastening together metal plates'. In its subsequent use, it largely retains a certain criminal or at least dodgy feel to it, so it's quite surprising to find that it was widespread in the West Riding of Yorkshire and in the areas of Lancashire bordering it in the 1880s and 1890s. Later evidence from these areas is hard to find, and the word provides an excellent example both of the potentially evanescent nature of slang and of the difficulties and unpredictabilities of trying to research the spread and development of non-standard language.

See MONEY TALKS – OR DOES IT? p. 144, *and also* ACKERS, GELT, MORGS, SPONDULICKS

rindle

stream, rivulet (north-west Midlands)

Rindle is a variant, with what linguists call an intrusive letter ('d' in this case), of an Anglo-Saxon word **rinnel**, which itself was a variant of **runnel**. The original word comes from **run**, as in 'running water'. Rindle is first recorded in the mid-sixteenth century, and within a century or so it had become localised to the area around Staffordshire, Cheshire, west Derbyshire and south Lancashire. The form **rundle**, harking back to the original word, has also been recorded in Cheshire. **Runnel** was still around in the early twentieth century when it was recorded in the *English Dialect Dictionary* (1905), chiefly in Yorkshire.

See WATER WATER EVERYWHERE, p. 170, *and also* BECK, BURN, NAILBOURN, PRILL, SIKE, STELL

s

sag

to play truant (Liverpool)

Sagging can still be heard in Liverpool as a code for skipping school. In Iona and Peter Opie's fascinating collection of the *Lore and Language of Schoolchildren* in the 1950s, the authors state emphatically that sagging 'is definitely the prevailing term [for playing truant] amongst delinquents in all parts of Liverpool'. The TV dramatist Alan Bleasdale also uses sagging in his Merseyside dramas. The origin is difficult to divine, but there may be a link with the Danish word *sakke*, which means 'to lag behind'. Or it may be a local development of the more widespread and earlier **wag**, which was common in Lancashire by the end of the nineteenth century.

See BUNKING AND PLUNKING, p. 192, *and also* BUNK OFF, DOG, MITCH, NICK OFF, PLUNK, PLAY HOOKEY, SKIDGE, SKIVE, TWAG, WAG

sannies

soft shoes (Scotland and the North-East)

Sandshoes, or **sannies** for short, have been around since the middle of the nineteenth century. This is the standard word in Scotland, and is also used in the North-East as far south as Hull. It describes shoes used for walking on sand, especially beach shoes with canvas uppers and soles of gutta-percha or hemp, which greatly resemble the traditional school gym shoe. In Glasgow the term is often used more generally for trainers, such as some 'mincy wee running sannies' worn by someone getting on the wrong side of Rab C. Nesbitt.

See ANYONE FOR SANNIES? p. 99, *and also* DAPS, GUTTIES, PUMPS

scald

to make tea (chiefly Staffordshire, Shropshire, Worcestershire and Yorkshire)

Although recorded sporadically all down the east coast from Northumberland to Kent, the epicentre of the use of **scald** runs from Staffordshire down to Worcestershire. In this area, it is used both transitively ('to scald the tea') and intransitively ('I'll go and scald'). Yorkshire is another area of common use, but only the transitive sense ('I scalded the tea') is recorded there. In the light of synonyms relating the making of tea to the brewing of beer, the fact that the *English Dialect Dictionary* collected scald in Yorkshire meaning 'to pour boiling water on malt in brewing' is probably significant in tracking down the term's origin, although evidence is a little too scanty to judge for certain.

See KETTLE'S ON, p. 185, *and also* BIRLE, EMPT, HELL, MASK, MASH, SOAK, TEEM, WET

scally

self-assured or roguish young person (chiefly Liverpool)

Shortened from **scallywag**, **scally** is used throughout Lancashire to describe a young working-class male, but in Liverpool it carries particular connotations of cockiness or of being a bit of a chancer. It frequently has less negative connotations than the other words employed to describe urban youth, at least when used by the mainstream media. The scally is definitely not a **chav**, but very much a rogue, and therefore, potentially at least, loveable. You don't have to look far to find most successful working-class Scousers described as scallies, especially musicians like the Beatles and footballers like Robbie Fowler and Steven Gerrard.

Kettle's on

To describe tea as brewing originally involved a direct analogy to the act of brewing beer. **Brew** is an Anglo-Saxon word, used by Alfred the Great, so beer had been brewed in England for almost a millennium by the time tea began to be in the nineteenth century. Brew quickly became established as the standard term for the process and dominant in the South, South-East and East Anglia. It developed both transitive ('brew the tea') and intransitive senses ('the tea is brewing'). Further north, the specific part of the brewing process most akin to making tea, the infusion of the malt in water, was used as the point of departure for these senses. It was known as **mashing** from the Midlands up to Yorkshire, and as **masking** in the north of England and in Scotland. In the South-West, the analogy with brewing was not used, with the more straightforwardly descriptive **soak** and **wet** gaining currency. In Hampshire the term is **bide and draw**, while in Warwickshire they **steep**.

Words for pouring tea, meanwhile, don't show quite the same level of variation as those for making or brewing it, but the variation they do show follows a very similar pattern. As with brew, pour is the dominant word in general across the South. In Cornwall they **ent**; in Cheshire they **lade** or **laden**. **Teem** is dominant in the North and covers broadly the same area as mash with two exceptions – the West Midlands and an area roughly corresponding to the East Riding of Yorkshire. Further north of that, where mask is used for brewing, pour returns. The South-West adds a few extras: **empt**, **hell** and **shoot** are found there instead of pour, just as soak and wet are for brew.

A fair lexicon, then, but then for such an important British pastime you wouldn't expect anything else.

See also BIRLE, EMPT, HELL, MASH, MASK, SCALD, SOAK, TEEM, WET

Scallywag itself has a lovely history. The term began as **scurryvag**, which came from a Latin phrase *scurra vagus* meaning 'a wandering fool or jester'. In London the word was used to describe a beggar or 'scurrilous vagrant', which in turn became trade union slang for a man who refuses to work or a political opportunist. A rogue has probably never had a more colourful name.

See THE CHAVS AND THE CHAV-NOTS, p. 43, *and also* CHARVER, CHAV, JANNER, KAPPA SLAPPER, NED, PIKEY, TROBO

Scotch mist

mist; something fanciful or unknown (Scotland)

A **Scotch mist** is, literally, a kind of thick mist characteristic of the Highlands, and it is mentioned as far back as the mid-seventeenth century. In Sir Walter Scott's *Waverley* (1814), the hero's aunt was said to have charged her nephew to 'beware of Scotch mists, which, she had heard, would wet an Englishman through and through . . . and, above all, to wear flannel next to his skin'.

From these literal beginnings the term also came to be used allusively, to denote something insubstantial or unreal, and also sarcastically to imply something that someone has imagined or not properly understood. Such a state might well be induced by the third sense of Scotch mist, which is a drink of whisky served with a twist of lemon.

Scouse(r)

Liverpudlian (UK-wide)

See LOBSCOUSE

shrammed

cold (the South and South-West)

> **Shrammed**, meaning 'cold or freezing', thus **all of a shram**, has
> been used throughout the rural south of England as far east as Sussex
> since the seventeenth century. The words of one Isle of Wight local
> were recorded at the beginning of the twentieth century: 'Let's get
> avore the fire, vor I be ver' neer shrammed.' As time has gone on, it
> has become more and more localised in the west.
>
> Shrammed may not appear to be linked to the shrimp, but it is.
> The root for both is an Old English verb **scrimman**, meaning 'to be
> paralysed' or 'to deprive someone of movement through a
> contraction of the muscles' (which in turn provided **shrim**, 'to
> shrink or shrivel'). The idea of shrinking works on various levels: in
> addition to the weather-induced sort, there is a link to scrimp, as in
> scrimp and save and, as promised, to the shrimp, which started life
> in Middle English as meaning any diminutive creature – so small, in
> fact, that it looks as though it's shrunk.
>
> We can find another link in West Somerset's **scram**, meaning
> 'abnormally small or insignificant-looking', 'puny' – hence 'a scram
> hand' describes a withered hand.
>
> Finally, **scram-handed** and **scrammed** mean 'to be paralysed'
> and, to come full circle, 'to be benumbed' (with cold).
>
> *See* BLOWING HOT AND COLD – MOSTLY COLD, p. 152, *and also* NESH,
> NITHERED, TATERS

sicker

safe (Scotland)

> Glasgow's **sicker**, meaning 'safe', is no more than a pronunciation of
> the standard English term 'secure' – this and other versions of the term
> go all the way back to the ninth century. The ultimate root is Latin
> *securus*, literally 'free of care'. In Northumberland **sicker** once meant
> 'wary' or 'sly', and was frequently prefixed by **gey**, an intensifier,
> meaning 'very', 'considerably', giving 'he's a gey sicker yen'.

How to talk like... **an Ulsterman**

There's a corny old joke told in Belfast about the boy who is found crying his eyes out beside a river. A passer-by enquires what's upset him, and the boy replies, 'Well, ah've droppt mi meiyt; 's in the revver.' The man jumps into the river, but emerges empty-handed: 'Scuse me, ah can't feind yer wee frieynd.' The boy starts to laugh, protesting that he hadn't been talking about his friend (mate) but his sandwich filling (meat): 'Ah said it's mi *meiyt*, nawt mi meiyt as in "huyman",' he says. 'It's the meiyt outta mi sandwich!' Boom-boom.

Yes, well it's not a great joke, I agree, but what it does tell you about the way Ulstermen and -women speak is that this rich and historic accent contains some surprising vowel sounds which can lead, even without a schoolyard joke, to confusion. And it's perfectly true that the words *meat* and *mate* are homophones – i.e. are identically pronounced – on the streets of Belfast. (And that schoolyard, incidentally, over here is pronounced with a twisted 'oo' sound that's close to the French 'u' in *tu* but with an extra little darkening at the beginning: 'skeuuylyarrd'.) Other vowels are on the move too – 'ay', as we've seen, tightens to 'eiy' ('peiynt' is what you apply to walls, if it's not 'peiyperr'), the long 'i' of *vine*, *height* and *sign* is here flattened to 'ay': 'vane', 'hate' and 'sane', while its short variety, found in *pin* and *Sinn Fein* is closer to 'pen' and 'Shenn Feiyn'. Famously the 'ow' sound in Gordon *Brown* and *Portadown* is sharpened to something akin to 'eye', thus, 'Brine' and 'Porrtadine'.

Ulster folk often append the word 'wee' to items, as in the joke above, 'yer wee frieynd', or 'your wee man'. But 'man' in this context would sound more like 'maan' with a stretched quality to the short 'a' sound. There's also another quality to these vowels – a sort of tweak in the tail – which gives the speech of urban Northern Ireland a particular zest, and which all those familiar with the pronouncements of Ulster politicians of one stripe or another (it makes no difference to the sound of their accent) will recognise. It means that, for instance, 'ee' has an extra little sting: 'steeil', 'feeil' and 'reeil' (for *steal*, *feel* and *real*).

Rhoticity is very evident in Northern Ireland; who can forget the sound of Ian Paisley shouting 'No surrender', with all those rasped out 'r's. Ulstermen and -women definitely do sound their 'r's.

There can also be a breathiness to Ulster 't's, particularly after the 's' sound, such that *straight* can come out sounding more like 'sthreiaght'; meanwhile there's also a tendency to drop the 't' sound from words that begin with 'th' – 'I think therefore I am' in Northern Ireland might be rendered simply 'Ay hink dareforr ay aam.' (Contrast the southern Irish way with these initial 'th's which is routinely to harden them up to a simple 't': 'Oi tink, darefor I am.'

Urban accents in Ulster tend to be sharper, zestier and faster-spoken, the rural sounds gentler and slower. But generalisations are always misleading, and while it's true that many Ulster folk insert a 'y' sound after the hard 'c' in words like *car* and *cart* and so on, to make a sound again quite similar to that found in the Republic, 'cyar' and 'cyart', many do not.

But the one thing that's absolutely recognisable across the Six Counties is the tune of the regional accent, which rises constantly in each sentence, in a version of what's sometimes referred to as 'upspeak', or the 'high-rising terminal' tune that's become very familiar from Australian and Southern Californian speech. It's the constant interrogative note of this speech pattern that makes it distinctive. And while the international version is likely to have spread from Down Under and the west of the USA, the Ulster variety – as that to be found, curiously, also in Bristolian speech from the west of England – is a naturally occurring local variety that's been around for centuries and is part and parcel of these local British dialects.

Sadly, and perhaps by association with the ceaseless stream of bad news that poured from Northern Ireland for decades before the completion of the peace process, the sound of the Ulster accent became synonymous with disaster and hatred, from both sides of the sectarian divide. It's unlikely, therefore, for a while yet that it will rise up the list of favourite British accents. Yet today, BBC Radio 4 has a regular national newsreader who speaks with a marked Ulster accent, alongside all the other varieties on offer from the station – is this a sign of a rehabilitation, perhaps?

You might be **broke to the bone** (embarrassed) to be seen **daundering** (wandering) about with a bottle of **Buckie** (tonic wine, favourite of alcoholics) in the **carryout** (or bag) you'd got from the off-licence. But you could just tell the **wee dump-rat** (hooligan) to keep their **wee neb** (nose) out of your business or you'd call a **Peeler** (policeman, still current slang), **so you would** [typical Ulster reinforcing repetition]. And so what if you were **quare** (very) **rubbered** (drunk)? It was **good craic** (fun) anyway, **dead-on** (fantastic). **Craic ninety** (very good indeed), in fact.

SIMON ELMES

sike

stream, rivulet (the North and Scotland)

A **sike** is now found predominantly in the very north of England, in Cumbria, Durham and North Yorkshire (compare to **stell**), but it has a wider range and until recently was common throughout an extended area including most of Yorkshire, the East Midlands and most of Scotland (but especially the historic Border towns like Selkirk, Melrose and Hawick). This geographical spread says one thing to the historian or historical linguist: Vikings! It corresponds to the Danelaw, the area in which the Vikings held power in England, and within which the Old Norse language exerted a powerful influence on the early development of English. *Sike* is a Norse word, and like many Norse words in English ending in a hard consonant, it had a counterpart in the South and West ending in a soft one, **sitch** (dike and ditch give an exact parallel, and rig and ridge show the same phenomenon). Sitch was still recorded in Shropshire and southern Cheshire in the late nineteenth century with the exact same meaning as sike. Historically, both words were typically used to describe streams acting as boundaries between fields.

See WATER WATER EVERYWHERE, p. 170, *and also* BECK, BURN, NAILBOURN, PRILL, RINDLE, STELL

sile

to rain heavily (the North)

Like many northern dialect terms, **siling** comes from the millennium-plus-old Danish invasion of Britain, and probably reflects the Scandinavian term *sila*, 'to flow gently, to pour with rain'. As well as meaning 'to pour with rain', it is found in English defined variously as 'to go, pass or move', 'to glide' and also 'to fall, sink or subside', 'to fall down in a swoon' or 'to faint away' and, of tears, 'to flow'. In food preparation it refers to passing liquids through a strainer (the strainer itself is a **sile**), 'to pour', 'to drip' and 'to allow a liquid to settle and produce sediment'. Quite a multi-purpose list for such a small word.

skank

an ugly girl (UK-wide but particularly Manchester)

> **Skank**, an import from the US – and probably ultimately from Caribbean English – has a variety of meanings, including a smelly girl, an 'easy' girl or actual whore, a repulsive person, or a problematic situation. Following the modern bad = good paradigm (as in wicked, bad, etc.), it can also be an affectionate term of address.

> *See* THE MIRROR CRACKED, p. 31, *and also* BUTTERS, DUFFY, FUSTY, LAIDLY, MINGER, MUNTER, OBZOCKY, RANK

skelp

to hit, to smack (Scotland and northern England)

> The word **skelping** probably evolved because of its sound: it does exactly what it says on the tin. To **skelp** someone is to 'have their hide', in other words, to hit them hard. In East Anglia, you would be kicking them even more violently. The *Oxford English Dictionary* includes a quote from a York play of 1440 which gives the idea: 'skelpe hym with scourges and with skathes hym scorne'.

skidge

to play truant (Paisley, Scotland and Northern Ireland)

> **Skidge** may be related to a Scottish term **skiddle**, meaning 'to move rapidly and lightly', and English **skidding** meaning 'to run'. Whatever its origin, **skidging school** has a nice, childlike alliteration to it, which might account for its longevity.

Bunking and plunking: playing truant

The number of words for truancy has risen rapidly since the beginning of the twentieth century. This is scarcely surprising given that mass education only really began with the Elementary Education Act of 1870 and that playing truant in a boarding school is no easy task. The act of playing truant from school is rarely named as such by schoolchildren themselves, rather it's the voices of authority who use truant, a word that began life in English in the thirteenth century as a word for a vagabond having travelled from France and the word *truand*, 'a gangster or mobster' (the very old Parisian *rue de la Grande Truanderie*, built in the heart of the medieval underworld district, translates literally as 'street of the heavy mob'). For those who truant, though, there is a rich lexicon of slang terms from which to choose, and many of them have very local roots. The earliest word for playing truant is **mitching**, which originally meant 'to steal'. Later, both **nick** and **to play hookey** were also derived from 'steal' words. The association was a popular one: steal itself has long had the meaning 'leave quietly, absent oneself' when combined with 'away' or 'off'. Indeed, having 'off' attached is a characteristic feature of many of these words – **bunk off**, **nick off**, **skive off**, etc. Those verbs that are transitive – in other words those that come with a direct object – are found either with 'school' as the object or just 'it'. So you can **wag school**, or **plunk** it, or vice versa. Probably the most general term for playing truant is **skiving off**, which originated among military personnel during the First World War, and was later picked up by schoolchildren.

See also BUNK OFF, DOG, MITCH, NICK OFF, PLUNK, PLAY HOOKEY, SAG, SKIDGE, SKIVE, TWAG, WAG

skimmished

drunk (Ireland and moving out through the UK)

'One night I went out with three other blokes for a drink. Of course we
ended up very happy. We were supposed to be back by 1200 hours.
Instead, I and two others got back late and stood outside the billet
singing "Old Father Thames". For that I got 14 days CB. I was with
Dutchy Holland. We were **skimmished**!' Or, as the officer on duty
doubtless put it, drunk. It would be his last drink for a while, since this
diary entry from a billeted soldier was written in the autumn of 1939.
The word skimmished itself comes from Shelta – the Irish tinker's
language – and the word **skimis**, which means 'to drink'. The *Oxford
English Dictionary*'s definition of the Shelta language may shed some
light on the origin of skimmished; it describes it as 'a cryptic jargon
used by tinkers, composed partly of Irish or Gaelic words, mostly
disguised by inversion or by arbitrary alteration of initial consonants'.

See LIQUID LUNCHES, p. 70, *and also* BLOOTERED, DRUCKEN, DRUFFEN,
FLUTHERED, MALLETED, PISHED, PUGGLED, STOCIOUS

skive (off)

to play truant (UK-wide but especially the South-East)

Skiving or **skiving off** is a term that has become widespread in
British English. Its origins are a little obscure, but it may come from
an older dialect meaning of the verb (found in Northampton and
Norfolk, for example) which was 'to move lightly and quickly'.
There may also be a link to the French verb *esquiver*, 'to dodge', 'to
slink away' (a synonym of which in some French dictionaries is *filer
à l'anglaise*, which when translated swaps national accusation to
become 'take French leave'). **Skive** in the sense of avoiding work or
a responsibility was originally British military slang from the First
World War. It had certainly arrived in schools by the time of the
Second World War, judging from printed sources, but it was
probably already spoken slang many years earlier.

See BUNKING AND PLUNKING, p. 192, *and also* BUNK OFF, DOG, MITCH, NICK
OFF, PLAY HOOKEY, PLUNK, SAG, SKIDGE, TWAG, WAG

skopadiddle

a mischievous child (Yorkshire)

This Yorkshire term, meaning 'a mischievous child', apparently started life in Sheffield, but has long since moved on.

Etymologically it is a poser, with a probable link to **skopperil** which the *English Dialect Dictionary* describes variously as a spinning top, a squirrel and 'a lively, restless person or animal; an active, agile child; a young rascal'. The most likely origin is that of the spinning top (incidentally, another term once aimed at children was **spinning like a teetotum**, another form of spinning top).

See TEARDOWN TEARAWAYS, p. 179, *and also* LISH, UNEASY, WAKEN, WICK, YAP

slammakin

slovenly (Devon)

Putting together the cast of 'women of the town' who provide the background to his *Beggar's Opera* (1727), the playwright John Gay simply 'christened' a bunch of synonymous slang terms through his characters. Thus among the companions of Macheath (the original Mack the Knife) are such as Diana Trapes, Dolly Trull, Betty Doxy, Nancy Jade, Carrie Shrew, Molly Braze and . . . Mrs Slammekin. The word was presumably old then, and meant, as it does now, 'slovenly', especially as regards dress. Indeed, as Macheath ironically said to Mrs S: 'Mrs. Slammekin! as careless and genteel as ever! all you fine Ladies, who know your own Beauty, affect an Undress'; in other words, they failed to smarten up.

The original **slammakin**, though, was not so much a dirty garment, but a long, loose one: presumably its dragging along unswept streets added the filth, and so the dirty garment came to signify its wearer. Nor is Mrs Slammekin merely grubby as to her dress. She is very fond, Gay adds, of a 'French' tune: a play on words in which French, as in so much slang, implies a connection with sex.

slob

mud (Ireland, Shropshire and Cheshire)

Like **slub**, **slob** is the soft mud often found on the seashore. In this form the word is mostly used in, or in reference to, Ireland, but it also has an extended form, **slobber**, which is the mud or slime produced by slushy, sleety rain or snow. What you end up with is a sloppy mess or mixture that resonates loudly from the word itself.

See MUD, MUD, GLORIOUS MUD, p. 196, *and also* CLART, PLODGE, SLUB, SLUCH

slub

mud (Cornwall and the South-West)

Slub perfectly captures the thick sludgy mud that sticks to your feet and that mixes in with sand and pebbles near the beach. One description of the mud-flats near Devon speaks of 'the gripes and gullies of the slub ooze'. You can't say it any better than that.

See MUD, MUD, GLORIOUS MUD, p. 196, *and also* CLART, PLODGE, SLOB, SLUCH

slutch

mud (UK-wide)

Slutch is still in used in Yorkshire and some parts of northern England. It is a variant of the more onomatopoeic **sludge** – the mud or ooze that covers the surface of the ground or the bottom of rivers.

See MUD, MUD, GLORIOUS MUD, p. 196, *and also* CLART, PLODGE, SLOB, SLUB

Mud, mud, glorious mud

The number of local versions of words for raining, and particularly drizzling, comes pretty high on dialect's scale (*see* DON'T TALK DRIZZLE, p. 10). Of course the inevitable result of so much British rain is that wonderfully sticky sucking substance beloved of all children. Mud is beautifully described in the *OED* as the 'soft, moist, glutinous material resulting from the mixing of water with soil, sand, dust, or other earthy matter'. It is a definition deserving of some onomatopoeic descriptors. And dialect certainly provides them.

See CLART, PLODGE, SLOB, SLUB, SLUCH

smeech

an unpleasant smell (Cornwall)

We all know about smooching, but would we also like a **smeech**? On the whole not, since it means 'an annoying smell', especially of burning. To smeech is 'to smoke', 'to give out dust', or 'to emit a nasty odour', while **smeechy** means 'scenting the air with an unpleasant smell'.

The word comes from Anglo-Saxon **smocan** meaning 'to emit smoke', 'to reek' or 'to send out or give off steam or vapour'. It is, of course, a close relative of today's word smoke. Finally, smeech can also mean 'to smoke out' things such as a wasp's nest, or 'to scent' somewhere, usually a church, with incense.

smirr

light rain (Scotland, Northern Ireland)

Smirr is the most widespread of the many Scottish synonyms for drizzle. It is first recorded in 1790, and was in its early days largely confined to southern Scotland. By the beginning of the twentieth century, it had broadened out into general Scottish use, with the variant **smirn** also found. The etymology is uncertain, but the occasional appearance of the word in East Anglia and Hampshire perhaps gives weight to the suggestion that it is simply imitative of the sound of persistent drizzle.

See DON'T TALK DRIZZLE, p. 10, *and also* BANGE, HADDER, MIZZLE

snap

a light snack (Nottinghamshire and in pockets across the UK)

Snap is recorded in most counties of England, but there is a slight predominance in the Midlands and North. In D. H. Lawrence's *Sons and Lovers*, Paul Morel's father takes bread and butter and some cold tea down the pit in his white calico **snap-bag**. The term's origin is the verb 'to snap', with the idea of a light meal eaten quickly. It is first recorded in the seventeenth century.

See CLOCKING UP YOUR CROUSTS, p. 214, *and also* BAG, BAIT, CLOCKING, JACKBIT, NUMMIT, TOMMY

snicket

alleyway (the North-West)

Snicket is equivalent to **ginnel** both in meaning and in the areas in which it is used. The word seems to have originated in Cumbria and to have travelled south to meet up with ginnel, which was moving north from south Lancashire.

See BY THE WAY, p. 126, *and also* ENNOG, ENTRY, GINNEL, JIGGER, LOAN, LOKE, TWITCHEL

snotter

to hit on the nose (Lancashire)

To snotter, in standard English, was once 'to snuffle or snort'. While this sense has died out, dialect's **snotter** survives in Lancashire and some other pockets of Britain where it means 'to deliver a blow to the snot-producer' (**snot**, incidentally, goes right back to the fifteenth century and was not always considered vulgar).

soak

to brew tea (the South-West)

Soak appears to be a relative newcomer to the group of words meaning 'to brew tea'. While the principle variants (**brew**, **mash**, **mask**, **scald** and **wet**) are all in place by the mid-nineteenth century, soak is not recorded until the middle of the twentieth. Both transitive ('I've soaked the tea') and intransitive ('the tea must soak a bit') are recorded in Cornwall, Devon, Dorset and Somerset. Curiously, synonyms such as soak, which don't make an analogy between making tea and brewing beer, are particularly common in the South-West.

See KETTLE'S ON, p. 185, *and also* BIRLE, EMPT, HELL, MASH, MASK, SCALD, TEEM, WET

soft

silly (Liverpool)

Apparently first used in this sense by the seventeenth-century scholar Robert Burton, in his *Anatomy of Melancholy*, **soft** meaning 'silly' or 'foolish' has a dual history – in formal literature (Trollope, Capt. Marryat and Fanny Burney, for example) and as part of informal dialect speech. It is recorded at some point in the local speech of practically all parts of the British Isles, but is now most commonly associated with Liverpool, especially in the phrase **soft lad** used as a form of address. It can be found in any modern Liverpool novel: for example, 'Aye soft lad, are you ready?' (*Brass*, by Helen Walsh). The Survey of English Dialects in the 1950s found the word particularly in Leicestershire and Norfolk.

Incidentally, in some parts of Britain, soft can mean stupefiedly drunk.

See DON'T BE DAFT, p. 189, *and also* ADDLE-HEADED, BARMY, DAFT, FOND, GORMLESS, QUILT

sorry

a friend, a mate (the Midlands)

In D. H. Lawrence's novel *Sons and Lovers*, set amid the collieries of Nottinghamshire, the hero's miner father is asked, 'Shall ter finish, **Sorry**?' by his fellow **butty**. These two terms for companion or mate were extremely popular in the Midlands and Lancashire and their mining communities. Sorry is a version of **sirrah**, which in turn derives from **sir** and the Old French *sire*. Its ultimate origin is the Latin *senior*, meaning 'elder'.

See also BLOOD, BREDREN, BUTTY, CATERCOUSIN, CHUCK, CLICK, CREW, GAFFER, HOMIE, MARRA, MUCKER

spell for

to hint at, to tell, etc. (in pockets across the UK)

Once upon a time . . . and indeed ever after, a **spell**, which took its roots in the Anglo-Saxon verb **spellian**, meaning 'to talk or discourse', was quite simply a story. It is exactly the same spell as the one that lies at the witch's evil heart of so many fairy tales. For dialect purposes it has slipped somewhat sideways and means 'to hint at obtaining', as in 'I could tell what he was spelling for'. But that is hardly its sole definition: uses in dialect include meaning 'to tell, inform, narrate or instruct', or their very opposite, namely 'to lie', or at least 'embellish one's account'. There are many more meanings besides. Casting a spell might take you anywhere.

spondulicks

money (in pockets across the UK)

Sounding like an escapee from a P. G. Wodehouse novel (and you can find it there), **spondulicks** (variously spelt as **spondulacks**, **spondulicks**, **spondooli** and **spondulix**, and abbreviated as **sponds**) is a good deal older even than Bertie Wooster. It is probably from a Greek word, *spondulikos*, which was a type of shell used as early money. It may be, though, and as pointed out by a correspondent to Michael Quinion's website World Wide Words, that the same Greek stem *spondylo-* is the source of various English words that refer to the spine or vertebrae. Perhaps then a stack of coins looked like the equivalent of the spine, with each coin representing another vertebra. There is some proof for this in an 1867 guide to writing for schools, which lists various regionalisms including 'Spondulics – coins piled for counting'.

See MONEY TALKS – OR DOES IT? p. 144, *and also* ACKERS, GELT, MORGS, REVITS

square

old-fashioned (UK-wide but particularly the South-East)

Like its antonym cool, **square** is a term that has a far longer history than you might think. It already had the meaning 'honest', 'truthful', 'fair', at least of a thing or idea, around 1650, and the image of respectability and honesty as far as a person was concerned appeared around 1800. From there it began to mean 'substantial', and then, around 1850, 'safe' and 'dependable' – from a criminal point of view, that is. The next century saw it progress to encompass sobriety and correctness. Finally, at least in the latest chapter of **square**'s story, in around the 1930s we find the modern use: conventional, conservative, naive and dull. And here it remains, other than on US campuses, where it can also mean 'straight' in the sense of heterosexual.

See also ANTWACKY

stell

stream, rivulet (Yorkshire and the North-East)

Since its first appearance in the mid-seventeenth century, **stell** has been associated strongly as meaning a 'stream' or 'brook', with the North Riding of Yorkshire, Durham, and the North-East as far as the Scottish Borders, although it is also recorded in Cumbria and the

West Riding. It is also sometimes used to mean 'an open ditch in a marsh'.

See WATER WATER EVERYWHERE, p. 170, *and also* BECK, BURN, NAILBOURN, PRILL, RINDLE, SIKE

stocious
drunk (Ireland)

Like **fluthered**, **stocious** originated in Southern Ireland in the early twentieth century, but it has become common in Northern Ireland too, where it can also be used as an adverb. For example, in Billy Roche's play *A Handful of Stars*, one character remembers when his father would have 'come in stocious drunk and gave me poor Ma a couple of belts'. No one quite knows its origin, although a 1949 collection of observations on Ireland talks about the various expressions for escalating degrees of intoxication: 'You have . . . spifflu, langers, and stocious. The last word rhymes with atrocious and means thickly speaking drunk . . . We were unable to find anybody who had ever seen it in print.' The following years soon put that right.

See LIQUID LUNCHES, p. 70, *and also* BLOOTERED, DRUCKEN, DRUFFEN, FLUTHERED, MALLETED, PISHED, PUGGLED, SKIMMISHED

stotty
bread roll (north-east England)

A **stotty** is a bread roll, or sometimes a larger flat round loaf, from the North-East, also called more fully a **stotty cake** or **stotty bun**. The word is often now distinctively applied to a **bap** or **cob**, sliced and filled with meat or cheese, and distinctively eaten by Geordies, **mackems**, and other North-Easterners. In this region bread that isn't a stotty is a **fadge**, meaning that it is fully risen with a round top.

The stotty's origins have been lost, but the plump roll might be stout, or you might stutter while attempting to talk with your mouth full of one.

See OUR DAILY BREAD, p. 49, *and also* BAP, BARM CAKE, BUTTY, COB, MAN-SHON, NUBBIES

stovies

potatoes (Scotland and northern England)

The *Oxford English Dictionary*'s first quotation for **stovies** is from 1893 and a collection of Northumberland words: 'Hey! lass, is the stavies [sic] no ready yit?' Stovies, or **stoved tatties**, are potatoes cooked in a pot (i.e. on the stove as opposed, presumably, to inside it). It is also a term for an Irish stew, for **stovy** itself means 'close' or 'hot'.

strapped

poor, skint (UK-wide)

Bereft of any income, you are **strapped** for cash. Strapped here applies a literal sense – the result is that you tighten the belt. Hence the imagery, although additionally in the nineteenth century **strap** could mean 'credit', which holds you together. An alternative etymology, dependent on images of emptying rather than of tightening, draws on the dialect use of strap to mean 'to drain dry', notably a cow's udder.

stream the clome

to do the washing up (Cornwall)

The nature of dialect often takes standard English terms and gives them a local twist. Sometimes, however, the words are local to begin with, part of an adjacent technology, whether or not it still exists. This is the case with the rich Cornish phrase for doing the washing up: **stream the clome**. **Clome** comes from the Old English term **clám**, meaning 'mud', and by extension 'potter's clay'. In household terms this equated with objects made of clay, thus 'earthenware pots'. As for **stream**, this comes from sixteenth-century Cornish tin-mining, and referred to washing the surface deposits of tin. From there it was adopted to describe the dipping of clothes into blueing water, and thence moved easily into meaning 'the washing up'.

swimy

giddy (the South-East)

> **Swimy** is a distinctively south-eastern version of **swimmy**, being widely recorded in Sussex and Kent. As such it represents one of the now very few cases where the South-East has a regional synonym that is not in line with the standard, or at least the dominant, southern word. Swimmy is comparable to the idea of 'my head is swimming' and is recorded in the nineteenth century in many parts of the country, but especially in the South, as well as in literary English.
>
> *See* GOING SWIMMINGLY, below, *and also* MAZY, REEZIE

Going swimmingly

When it comes to feeling unsteady and light-headed, there is a distinct North–South divide. Draw a line from the border of Shropshire and Cheshire to about halfway up the Essex coast, say Brightlingsea: north of that line, people are **dizzy**, south of it **giddy**. The principal alternatives are **mazy** in the North-West, and **swimy** (or **swimmy**) in the South (which like most of these can have -headed stuck on the end, as can the more sparsely recorded **whirly** and **wonky**).

There are a few wonderful local alternatives, such as **drumlie** in Scotland, **fuddled** and **head-light** in Cornwall, **whirly** in Surrey and **wonky** in Derbyshire and Yorkshire.

See also MAZY, REEZIE, SWIMY

taid

grandfather (Wales)

> From the Welsh word for grandfather, **taid** is found in all parts of Wales. The form **tadcu** is also found in the west, where the Welsh language is strongest. Taid has also been recorded on the other side of the border in Shropshire.

> *See* 'GRANDAD, GRANDAD . . .', p. 93 *and also* GRAMP, GRANFER, GRANSHER, GUTCHER

tale-pyet

a gossip (Cumbria)

> **Tale-pyets** were around (in name at least) in Yorkshire in the eighteenth century and subsequently up to the Scottish Borders. In the Survey of English Dialects, the term was collected in Cumbria. The second element **pyet** ultimately means 'magpie' and is an old northern variant of pie. There is a long history of words associating talkative or chattering people with magpies, going back at least to the thirteenth century, when pyet is found with the sense of a 'talkative person, gossip'.

> *See* ALL THE LOCAL GOSSIP, p. 34, *and also* CANK, CANT, CHAMRAG, CLISH-MA-CLAVER, COOSE, JAFFOCK, JANGLE, NEIGHBOUR, PROSS

tatchy

moody, bad-tempered (the South-West)

A variant of **tetchy**, recorded in Lincolnshire and east Yorkshire at the end of the nineteenth century, but most characteristically in the South-West, **tatchy** sounds just as it feels: scratchy. In the words of one Devonian of the end of the nineteenth century: 'I niver zeed zich a tatchy, ill-contrived little twoad in awl my life.'

See THE MARDY BLUES, p. 134, *and also* COB ON, MARDY

taters

cold (Cockney)

Taters, or **potatoes in the mould**, or **taters in the mould**, is Cockney rhyming slang, and like most examples of this type of word is relatively recent, being first recorded in the 1930s. Like many Cockney rhyming slang words, it has spread into more general use mainly in its shortened form. It seems to have come to wider prominence in the 1970s, probably under the influence of TV shows that popularised a lot of London talk, including rhyming slang, such as *The Sweeney* and *Porridge*.

See BLOWING HOT AND COLD – MOSTLY COLD, p. 152, *and also* NESH, NITHERED, SHRAMMED

teem

to pour tea (northern England)

Common in Yorkshire (except the East Riding), Lancashire, Durham, Westmorland, and north Cheshire and Lincolnshire, **teem** is the principal verb in the North for pouring a brew. It derives from an old Scandinavian word and is recorded with the general sense of 'emptying a vessel' from the thirteenth century, and in northern dialect with specific reference to pouring out tea from the early nineteenth century.

See KETTLE'S ON, p. 185, *and also* BIRLE, EMPT, HELL, MASH, MASK, SCALD, SOAK, WET

thirl

hole or opening (Cornwall, Devon and West Somerset)

> **Thirl** derives from an Anglo-Saxon word meaning 'hole' and gives
> us the second part of nostril (literally 'nose hole'). It is still very
> much in evidence in the South-West where it can refer to any kind
> of hole or opening, be it a door in a building, a closet or a hole that
> has been bored into a surface. In mining language, a thirl was a
> passage built through the wall of the mines, also known as the
> **thurlings** or **thirlings**.

thock

to pant (Northumberland)

> **Thock** is in many ways a perfect dialect word: it is evocative,
> somewhat odd-looking and obscure in origin. It has been collected
> exclusively in Northumberland, first in 1850 in Thomas Bewick's *The
> Howdy and the Upgetting* (which provides a good example of its
> Geordie evocativeness – 'Here cums little Andra Karr . . . thockin
> and blowin'), and later in the Survey of English Dialects in the
> 1950s. The initial 'th-' and final '-ck' are also characteristic of the
> region and combine to give it an almost Anglo-Saxon feel. But its
> etymology is completely unclear and there is simply not enough
> evidence to allow us to speculate anything less than wildly about it.

> *See* A PILE OF PANTS, p. 209, *and also* PANK, TIFT

thrape

to beat a child as punishment (chiefly West Midlands and East Wales)

> **Thrape** is unusual among words for beating a child in that it didn't
> start out as a verb meaning 'to hit' but rather one that originally
> meant 'to rebuke, reprove'. It is an Anglo-Saxon word whose
> standard form was **threap**, and which has traditionally been found
> mainly in Scotland and the North. It is, however, in the area either
> side of the Welsh border that the specific context of punishing

children has been most common, and in that region it is recorded in the distinctive form thrape.

See A TWANK AND A WALLOP, p. 15, *and also* BENSIL, MOLLYCRUSH, TWANK

thrawn

bad-tempered (Scotland and northern England)

Thrawn, meaning 'ill-tempered' or 'cantankerous', is the Scottish and northern form of standard English's thrown, meaning 'twisted', particularly in the context of turning wood on a lathe. Thrawn is usually found in reference to the mouth, in such compounds as **thrawn-faced**, -**gabbit**, -**mowit**, all meaning having a thrawn or twisted face or mouth – in other words one that is crabbed, ill-tempered or snarling. One *Oxford English Dictionary* quote from the prolific Scottish novelist Samuel Crockett carries the ultimate line in insult: 'Ye thrawn-faced, slack-twisted muckle haythen ye.'

tickety boo

fine and dandy (originally the South but now UK-wide)

When something is **tickety boo**, it is in order or satisfactory. The precise origin of the phrase is uncertain, but one theory is that it stems from a Hindi phrase *tikai babu* meaning 'it's all right, sir', and that it was imported into English by the British Army. The first mention of the term in the *Oxford English Dictionary* is from 1939, but Eric Partridge, a major chronicler of British slang, contended that tickety boo was widely used in the British forces – and in particular in the RAF – during the 1920s.

One further possibility is that the term is an extension of the phrase 'that's the ticket', which may in turn refer to a winning lottery ticket.

Whatever its origin, tickety boo has an unmistakably old-fashioned feel to it – one very much stamped with the Britain of the 1930s and 40s.

tift

to pant (Cumbria and north Lancashire)

> **Tift** was used from the eighteenth century in southern Scotland as a noun meaning 'a gust of wind', and the localisation of this verb to the far north-west of England suggests it is related. The subsequent development of its meaning in Scots shows that it became strongly influenced by **tiff**, meaning 'quarrel', but the ultimate origin of the word probably lies in its sound, and its later use in Westmorland to mean 'to cough' reinforces this theory.

> *See* A PILE OF PANTS, below, *and also* PANK, THOCK

A pile of pants

While **pant** itself is of medieval French origin and entered English in the mid-fourteenth century, the key word in its history is really **puff**. Puff imitates the sound of blowing breath out from the lips and is recorded in Anglo-Saxon in the sense 'to emit a puff of air'. At least half a century before the first appearance of pant, it had developed the same sense of 'breathe hard'. For centuries, **to puff and blow** was the principal alternative to pant; by the eighteenth century **to puff and pant** was also common.

The local words that describe panting generally fall into two basic categories: some, like **bellows** (from Suffolk), **heave** (from Essex) and **pump** (from Staffordshire), are descriptive, but others, such as **huff** (from East Anglia), **tift** (from the North-West) and **waff** (from Yorkshire), can be seen as having puff as an ancestor on account of their imitative qualities (while **lall** from Lincolnshire suggests the tongue lolling out in the heat, like that of a dog).

Even **bussock**, recorded in Gloucestershire, might have an imitative origin. It is recorded earlier in Worcestershire with the meaning 'to cough', and it may be that it was originally imitative of coughing before extending its meaning to 'panting' (the reverse, in fact, of what happened with tift).

See also PANK, THOCK, TIFT

How to talk like ... a Cockney

'Applied only to one borne within the sound of Bow-bell': the classic definition of a Cockney was articulated by John Minsheu in 1617, and is still strictly so interpreted today. Yet for centuries the term has been loosely applied to the speech of anyone who hails from the capital and has a local accent. The word 'cockney' itself is fascinating and was once applied not just to Londoners, but to urban-dwellers in general by their rural compatriots who thought them to be more effete than their own hard-working sons of the soil. Even earlier, a 'coken-ey' or 'cock's egg' was the term for an infertile one, and thus applied to something inferior or inadequate. Today, Cockney has thrown off much of its stigma of inadequacy – though Bernard Shaw's Eliza Doolittle (*Pygmalion*, 1912) was roundly condemned for speaking the language of Covent Garden porters. Today, the Cockney accent, or a watered-down form of it, has become a national norm for the upwardly mobile (Lord Sugar, Greg Dyke, Janet Street-Porter, to name but three) in the form of so-called Estuary English.

In fact, so ubiquitous has a form of Cockney become on the streets of Britain, that we sometimes forget how sharp and abrasive the true form of the accent is. *Round* is classically pronounced 'raaend' (while in the softened Estuarial form it's more like 'raound') and the acid 'eye' for 'ay' vowel shift (where *basically* becomes 'bye-sickly') has in the gentler form of London speech stayed closer to 'baye-sickly'.

But other forms have softened less. 'Ow' in Received Pronounciation is familiarly rendered as 'aa' ('Lime-aahse' – Limehouse – is a well-known part of the East End) and the use of 'f' for 'th' (known by linguists as TH-fronting) is equally omnipresent; so Southend, the Essex resort beloved of East Enders, is routinely 'saafend'. Other vowels get the squeeze too – short 'a' becomes almost an 'e' (Caemden, Laembith – *Camden, Lambeth*), and, as in that last example, short 'e' can narrow towards a short 'i', while the 'uuh' sound in standard *girl* gets routinely shortened to a sort of semi-aspirated 'gehl' (a long way from the posh version of the same shift where a *very nice girl* is a 'veh naace gel').

As an urban accent, Cockney has all the features of big-city dialects – it's fast and rapped out with words tumbling and slurring together and the ubiquitous 'uh' sound (representing 'of') gluing everything together. Stand beside your average fruit-and-veg seller on the capital's streets and those run-together London syllables become almost incantatory: 'Sixty-pance-d'buhnaahnuhs-naace-raap-buhnaanuhs-faw-fuh-two-paahnd! Laavly straws, paahnduhpaahne'!' ('Sixty pence, the bananas. Nice ripe bananas. Four for two pounds! Lovely strawberries, a pound a punnet').

No time in this on-rush of words for 'h's in London, and the information that a patient has recently been taken to Northwick Park Hospital could well be reported: ''e's in 'ospi'ul in 'Arraow'. Those elusive London 'h's were the basis for a Victorian linguistic self-improvement morality tale called 'Poor Letter H' and they also beset Eliza Doolittle in the musical version of *Pygmalion*, *My Fair Lady* ('My Fair' is an accent-pun on *Mayfair*, too). So Eliza tries so hard to enunciate the phrase that Professor Higgins has given her about the 'rine in spine' – er, rain in Spain – because 'in Hertford, Hereford and Hampshire, hurricanes hardly ever happen'.

No time in London either for inconvenient little 't's in the middle of words. The London tumble has produced the glottal stop or unpronounced consonant 't' in words like *bottle*, *butter* and *bitter*. So on the Cockney's lips the familiar tongue-twister about Elizabeth's butter-buying exploits would be well and truly mangled: 'Be''y bough' bu''uh bu' duh bu''uh wuz bi''uh, so Be''y bough' be''uh bu''uh tuh mek duh bi''uh bu''uh be''uh' ('Betty bought butter but the butter was bitter, so Betty bought better butter to make the bitter butter better').

So powerful is the influence these days of London speech that to list Cockney terminology is in many ways to bring together much of the nation's vernacular. Thus a Cockney greeting his mate would use terms that the Arthur Daleys of this world have made nationally famous, such as **wotcha me ol' cock** (from cock-sparrow), slung together with assorted lumps of more local rhyming slang, **barnet** for hair (Barnet Fair) or **Hank Marvin** for hungry (starvin'). He might complain that his mate had been not entirely truthful: 'you bin tellin' **porkies**, aincha?' (pork-pies = lies) or that he was **potless** or **brassic** (broke). He might ask after the other's **nan** (grandmother) or report that everything was pretty **cushty** (in good order). His mate might tell him not to be a **berk** (idiot, vulgar rhyming slang from 'Berkshire Hunt') and confess he's feeling **cream-crackered** (originally another piece of not so decent rhyming slang for knackered, itself a piece of London usage for exhausted that's now found its way across the country). His favourite pastime might be a game of **arrers** (arrows = darts) at which he showed a lot of **bottle** (courage). All in all, they are, they conclude, a couple of **diamond geezers** (solid, reliable blokes).

SIMON ELMES

timber-toed

pigeon-toed (Nottinghamshire, Derbyshire and Cheshire)

Originally, a **timber toe** was a man with a wooden leg. The term is used in one of a number of celebrated works in Lancashire dialect from the middle of the eighteenth century written under the pseudonym 'Tim Bobbin'. The adjective form **timber-toed** is found later that century, and evidence for the metaphorical extension of its meaning to 'pigeon-toed' was collected in the 1870s by a philologically minded parson in South Cheshire. Subsequently, this sense has also been recorded in Staffordshire (where there is also another version, **timble-toed**), Derbyshire and Nottinghamshire.

See PIGEON ENGLISH, p. 218, *and also* TROLL-FOOTED, TWANG-TOED, TWILLY-TOED

tittamatorter

a seesaw (East Anglia)

East Anglia is full of terms for what is generally known as a seesaw. There is **tittamatorter**, **teeter-cum-tauter**, **titticumtawta** and **titty-ma-torter**. Other counties are just as keen: **teter-cum-tawter** can be found across the North and **tittem-a-tauter** in Warwickshire. Meanwhile, in the US, you can find **teeter-totter**. Only Durham, it would seem, breaks the style: there the seesaw is a **shig-shog**. Disappointingly, no obvious origin for the terms exist aside from the idea of teethering and lottering, although there is likely to be a link with **titt up**, a now obsolete phrase meaning 'to pull up'. It may also be a successor to a wonderful fifteenth-century Yorkshire term for a swing or a seesaw: a **merry-totter**.

tizzacky

wheezing, asthmatic (Derbyshire and East Midlands)

Devotees of Victorian novels will have probably encountered at least one hapless heroine ravaged by the horrors of **phthisis**. This barely pronounceable word, based on the Greek *phthino*, means 'to consume oneself' and refers to a variety of diseases which cause coughing fits, including asthma or bronchitis. It is this that is at the root of the Derbyshire and East Midlands term **tizzacky**. Also spelt **tissacky**, it means asthmatic, wheezing or coughing, and is the adjectival form of **tissick/tizzick**, a dry and/or hacking cough. And while the ultimate root is phthisis, a near relation is France's *tisique*, 'consumption', and presumably *tousser*, 'to cough'.

In some places **phthisicky** persisted, in spite of its unpronounceability. An ad in the *Kingston* (Jamaica) *Daily Gleaner* of 1931 declared that 'whenever you get a phthisicky cough you will do well to lose no time but get a bottle of Solomon's Lung Balsam'.

togs

clothes; swimming costume (UK-wide but particularly London and the South-East)

Much more recent than **clouts**, **rags** or **weeds**, **togs** probably ultimately derive from the Roman toga. The term first appears in the late eighteenth century as the plural of **tog**, which meant 'coat'. Tog was a shortened form of **togeman**, a word from criminal slang meaning 'loose coat or cloak' – which one quotation in the *Oxford English Dictionary* from 1718 describes as being 'in vogue among thieves' – and which was probably derived from the French word *toge*, itself a survival of the Latin *toga*.

Togs seems to have retained the underworld associations implied by its cant history until the end of the nineteenth century; it is, for example, used by Fagin in *Oliver Twist*. From after the First World War, though, it began to acquire the further specific, and much more domesticated, meaning of 'swimming costume', originally in Australia and New Zealand. For the British, however, your **togs** are more often than not simply your clothes.

Clocking up your crousts

The packed lunch is a common part of life, whether it be a couple of carpet-fitters or plasterers breaking off from the job to have lunch in the van, a schoolchild desperately hoping their mum or dad hasn't put a stick of celery in there again, or even an office worker looking for a cheaper alternative to the sandwich shop or café.

Given the variety of eaters, you might expect more regional variants than there in fact are. Nowadays they will be eating a packed lunch, perhaps a **pack lunch**, in North America sometimes a **sack lunch**. Go back a century or more, however, and the situation was quite different. Rural labourers in the field ate something quite specific when they opened their bags in the late morning. They still do; it's just that there's not so many of them now. Two main trends are visible in what these people ate. Some names are literal, referring directly to food (e.g. **morsel**) or to the fact of the food being packed (e.g. **bagging**). More interesting are the array of terms which refer to the time when the meal was taken, from specific times like **eleveners** (Cornwall), **elevens** (Essex), **threeses** (Suffolk), **nineses** (East Anglia), **tenner**

tommy

packed lunch (Herefordshire and south-east Wales)

> **Tommy** is a word that seems to have been slowly working its way round to the meaning of a 'packed lunch' or 'light snack'. It had been used in a number of areas, including Devon, in the nineteenth century to mean 'a loaf of bread', and at the beginning of the twentieth century it is recorded in Shropshire referring to a meal of bread and cheese. In the period between 1870 and 1905, a **tommy bag** was a bag in which a labourer or schoolboy from Somerset or the south-west Midlands took their lunch to work or school. Today, it is particularly in south-east Wales that the contents of that bag are known as a tommy.
>
> *See* CLOCKING UP YOUR CROUSTS, *above, and also* BAG, BAIT, CLOCKING, JACKBIT, NUMMIT, SNAP

(Hampshire) and **ten o'clock** (the North), through general references to time (**clocking, clocks** in Yorkshire), to those where the time in question, usually noon, is concealed in the first syllable (**nummit**).

Then there is **bagging(s)** (north-west Midlands), the glorious **biting on** (Yorkshire), **crib** (Cornwall and Devon), **croust** (Cornwall), **dew-bit** (Essex), **docky** (East Anglia), **drinking(s)** (Lancashire and Yorkshire) **drum-up** (Cheshire), **forenoons** (Somerset), **four o'clock** (Berkshire), **fourses** (East Anglia), **jawer** (Gloucestershire), **lowance** (Yorkshire), **morsel** (Cornwall), **nuncheon** (South Midlands), **packing** (Yorkshire), **progger** (Kent), **putting-on** (Yorkshire), **scran** (Lincolnshire) and **snack-bit** in (Shropshire).

One thing labourers didn't eat, even the ploughmen, was a ploughman's lunch. The earliest description of one in the *Oxford English Dictionary* is not until 1957 in the *Monthly Bulletin* of the Brewers' Society: 'There followed a "Ploughman's Lunch" of cottage bread, cheese, lettuce, hard-boiled eggs, cold sausages and, of course, beer.' But that isn't to say that a ploughman wouldn't have had some of these things, especially bread and cheese, in his nummit or clocking.

See also BAG, BAIT, CLOCKING, JACKBIT, NUMMIT, SNAP, TOMMY

---

trobo

young person in trendy clothes and flashy jewellery (Wiltshire)

Like **janner**, **trobo** has emerged from the trend of using an established colloquial term for an inhabitant of a town or city to describe the members of its youth subculture. **Townie** is used generally for this purpose, especially in Lancashire, but **trobo** is an extreme local form of it, used in Wiltshire to describe young people from Trowbridge.

See THE CHAVS AND THE CHAV-NOTS, p. 43, *and also* CHARVER, CHAV, JANNER, KAPPA SLAPPER, NED, PIKEY, SCALLY

troll-footed

pigeon-toed (Cornwall)

> **Troll** seems always to have been a distinctively Cornish word. In the nineteenth century, troll is recorded as a verb meaning 'to twist or sprain', **trolled** as an adjective meaning 'deformed', **troll-foot** as a noun meaning 'club foot', and troll-footed meaning 'club-footed'. The current use of troll-footed is without doubt an extension of that use. Indeed, the association between club feet and pigeon toes has also been made in Lancashire, where club-footed is recorded with the meaning 'pigeon-toed'.
>
> *See* PIGEON ENGLISH, p. 218, *and also* TIMBER-TOED, TWANG-TOED, TWILLY-TOED

trollies

women's underwear; trousers (Lancashire and London, and becoming widespread)

> **Trolly** was originally a kind of lace, perhaps from Flanders. By the end of the nineteenth century, the word had made the unsurprising journey to referring to a lace garment, and, in the plural, to women's drawers or knickers. Recorded earliest in Blackburn in 1891, the two focal points of its use seem to be Lancashire (for example in the letters of Blackburn-raised opera singer Kathleen Ferrier) and in girls' public schools (it is included in the diary of Barbara Pym). Over the course of the twentieth century, **trollies** came to mean 'trousers' without respect to gender, a process that might have started in Lancashire.

in tucks

in stitches, having fits of laughter (North Wales)

> If an audience is **in tucks** it is rolling in the aisles, but while the image may be of the tucks in one's stomach as you convulse with roars of mirth, such popular etymology is very far from the truth.

For this sense of **tuck** is rooted in the Italian *tocco*, defined by the sixteenth-century lexicographer John Florio as 'a stroke or knock, also a stroke of a bell or clocke' itself. The original English use was to describe the blast of a trumpet, and from there tuck became a blow, stroke or tap, typically as a **tuck of drum**. The sound of that musical noise clearly once conjured up the loud guffaw of laughter.

twag

to play truant (Hull and Doncaster)

Twagging may simply be an elision of **wagging**, but one citation included in the *Oxford English Dictionary* suggests it has been around as a dialect term for much longer. Robert Greene, in his 1592 pamphlet on **Coney-catching** (i.e. Elizabethan confidence trickery), wrote, 'Their word for knowing each other, as is said, was **Quest**, and this villaines comfortable newes to them, was **Twag**, signifying he had sped.' In playground slang meanwhile, a **twag officer** once denoted a truant officer.

See BUNKING AND PLUNKING, p. 192, *and also* BUNK OFF, DOG, MITCH, NICK OFF, PLAY HOOKEY, PLUNK, SAG, SKIDGE, SKIVE, WAG

twang-toed

pigeon-toed (Yorkshire and Lancashire)

Twang is a northern dialect word, probably related to tang and pang, whose senses are to do with pointedness. It is especially used of a sudden acute pain, or of something twisted. **Twang-toed** fits either with 'pointy' synonyms like **hook-toed** and **pincer-toed**, or with the slightly more negative sense of ungainliness found in **cleeky-feet** and **troll-footed**.

See PIGEON ENGLISH, p. 218 *and also* TIMBER-TOED, TROLL-FOOTED, TWILLY-TOED

Pigeon English

The vast array of descriptive terms referring to people whose feet point slightly towards each other as they walk can be attributed to the fact that, until the nineteenth century, there was no strong standard word in English. Looking at the list below, it isn't difficult to see that pigeon-toed looks very much like many of the other regional options, such as **chicken-toed** and **crow-toed**. Like those, its simple descriptiveness is striking.

Shall I compare thee to a summer's day? Sadly, the vast majority of bow-legs and inward-turning feet are compared to a bird. Pigeon-, chicken- and crow- all belong here, and duck-, goose- and turkey- are also found. There is some overlap between words meaning 'pigeon-toed' and those meaning 'splay-footed'. **Spraw-footed** is recorded as 'pigeon-toed' in Lancashire and Somerset, while **sprawl-footed** means 'splay-footed' in East Wales. Similarly, **duck-footed** is 'pigeon-toed' in Surrey, but 'splay-footed' in the north of England. The first is readily explainable, since spraw(l) is just the common word with various senses to do with ungainly movement. As for the second, do ducks walk differently in the South and the North?

There are a host of other terms too up and down the country. They include **chicken-toed**, **club-footed** (Lancashire), **cleeky-feet**, **crab-footed**, **crab-toed** (Northumberland), **crib-footed** (Staffordshire), **crow-toed** (Lincolnshire, Huntingdonshire), **duck-feet** (Leicestershire), **duck-nebbed** (Northumberland), **duck-toed** (Durham), **hen-toed** (South Midlands), **hook-toed** (Huntingdonshire), **keb-footed**, **keb-legged**, **nebbed**, **nebby**, **neb-footed** (Cumbria), **peg-toed** (Westmorland), **pincer-toed** (Lancashire, Yorkshire), **pumple-footed** (Somerset), **tip-toed** (Lincolnshire, Somerset), **toes-in**, **tosie** (Lancashire), **turkey-toed** (Cheshire), **turn-toed** (Shropshire), and **web-footed** (Durham).

See also TIMBER-TOED, TROLL-FOOTED, TWANG-FOOTED, TWILLY-TOED

twank

to hit, beat (northern England)

> **Twank** is an imitative word that starts like a twang, but comes to an abrupt end as does, for example, a hand, belt or any other available item when it comes into contact with a child's bottom. Smack probably ultimately shows the same kind of derivation. The word is principally found in Northumberland, Cumbria and Yorkshire. At the end of the nineteenth century, a Cumbrian man recalling his school days wrote: 'T'maister used t'twank them when they gat him on his ire.' Ouch.

> _See_ A TWANK AND A WALLOP, p. 15, _and also_ BENSIL, MOLLYCRUSH, THRAPE WALLOP

twilly-toed

pigeon-toed (East Midlands and Yorkshire)

> The verb **to twill** is found in Derbyshire and Yorkshire with the sense of 'turning the toes in', and it may be the only simple word (as opposed to a phrase or compound) that was coined specifically to describe pigeon toes. It probably goes back ultimately to the diagonal ridges on twilled cloth, and is therefore a descriptive term in origin. The alternative version **twill-toed** is recorded in Lincolnshire, while **twinny-toed** is still alive in Derbyshire.

> _See_ PIGEON ENGLISH, p. 218, _and also_ TIMBER-TOED, TROLL-FOOTED, TWANG-TOED

twirlies

pensioners; the elderly in general (Liverpool)

Twirlies is the name given to pensioners by Liverpool bus crews. Free bus passes become effective at 9am, but if the said pensioners arrive before this, they apparently enquire 'Are we too early?' hence the contraction **twirlie**. Elisions, whereby two words are blended into one, are a popular slang device, as seen in the recent **fugly** ('fantastically ugly'; the 'f' can stand for many coarser words), or **daks** (an Australian term for trousers, from 'dad's slacks'). Twirlies appears for the moment to be restricted to Scouse dialect, as does the more sinister term **tabbies**, another word for the elderly who are particularly vulnerable to being mugged (and have been **tabbed**).

twitchel

alleyway (East Midlands)

Imagine you wanted to cross the country from Preston to the Wash using only alleyways. The first half of your journey would be taken through **ginnels**, but once into Derbyshire, you would have to find a **twitchel** in order to carry on. Apparently deriving from an Anglo-Saxon word meaning 'fork in the road', twitchel is probably second only to **mardy** as a characteristic East Midlands word. It is first recorded in Nottingham in the fifteenth century ('the door that goes into the twitchel between the Shambles [i.e. butchers] and the Drapery'), and is common in Lincolnshire and Leicestershire as well as in Derbyshire. In addition, it is found in Yorkshire, east of the area in which ginnel is found.

See BY THE WAY, p. 126, *and also* ENNOG, ENTRY, GINNEL, JIGGER, LOAN, LOKE, SNICKET

tyke

a Yorkshireman (northern England)

Once applied as a derogative, but now embraced – as so often is the case – by its hitherto victims, **tyke** is the best-known nickname for a Yorkshireman. It started off its life as a word for a dog, usually a mongrel or cur, and was then transferred to humans, denoting a lazy, mean, surly or ill-mannered fellow. The Yorkshire connection is not entirely clear-cut. Perhaps the name was originally used with contempt before becoming a rather playful term taken on by Yorkshiremen themselves. Or it may be because in Yorkshire, unlike the majority of England, **tyke** is still a common word for a dog. There are further suggestions too: including Old Welsh **taiawc**, a 'peasant' or 'churl', and Cornish **tioc** or **tiac**, a 'husbandman', 'farmer', 'ploughman' or 'rustic'. Given that these are both some distance from Yorkshire, the dog may well have it. (A terrier, perhaps?)

umblement

an amount that is just about sufficient, but no more (Kent and the South-East)

> The **umbles** that originally went into **umbles pie** and which were later playfully converted to humble pie were the entrails of deer, given to the peasants at a dinner while their loftier fellow guests were served the meat. Kent's **umblement** may hark back to that bare nutrition, or it may simply be a contraction of humble amount. Whatever its origin, it manages to convey in a word what it takes standard English a sentence or two to deliver.

uneasy

(of a child) active (north of England, especially Cumbria)

> **Uneasy** used in this way seems to be a survival of a medieval sense of the word, namely 'difficult, troublesome', and which was common until about a century ago before fading from use. **Bothersome** in Manx English has the same history.

> *See* TEARDOWN TEARAWAYS, p. 179, *and also* LISH, SKOPADIDDLE, WAKEN, WICK, YAP

urchin

hedgehog (chiefly Yorkshire, Cumbria and Welsh borders)

Ultimately all **urchins** are hedgehogs. The word derives from the Norman French word *hurcheon* (of which the modern French *herisson* is a later form), which in turn derives from the Latin word for hedgehog, *hericius*. The word entered the English language in the fourteenth century, with its modern meaning (as in 'street urchin') not appearing for another 200 years. In its original meaning of 'hedgehog', urchin is now largely restricted to two areas. One is northern, including Cumbria, Lancashire, Yorkshire and Lincolnshire, and is characterised by often having **prickly** before it, such as **prickly urchin**, **prickly-back urchin**, and so on. The other area of use runs along both sides of the Welsh border, and as far east as Staffordshire. The original sense of the word has survived in standard English too, in the name of another animal – the sea urchin. Indeed, sea hedgehog was formerly an alternative name for this creature.

See COUNTRY URCHINS, below

Country urchins

The word hedgehog is an obvious English compound, deriving from **hedge** and **hog** (i.e. pig). It isn't surprising that people have historically created new variations by simply replacing one or both of these elements. So, hog has become boar and pig. **Hedgepig** is used by Shakespeare in *Macbeth* and is now still alive and well in the Home Counties and north-east Wales, while **prickly pigs** roam in Yorkshire, and **hedgyboars** can still be found in Devon. The main variant, however, is **urchin**, which derives from the Old French for hedgehog, *hurcheon* (still a word, incidentally, in Scotland and some parts of northern England).

See also URCHIN

wabbit

tired (Scotland)

Wabbit means 'tired out', or 'off colour', and is very much associated with Scottish English. Given its expressiveness, it is frustrating that its origin is unknown. The *Scottish National Dictionary* suggests that wabbit may be related to the word **woubit**, 'a hairy caterpillar', and a word sometimes contemptuously applied to a person. In this sense wabbit may have arisen from the slowness of a caterpillar's movement, suggesting heaviness and exhaustion.

John Buchan used a version of wabbit in his 1922 novel *Huntingtower*, in the account of how some of the little boys, the Gorbals Diehards, foil a Russian anarchist and his gang: 'When he had run round about them till they were wappit, he out with his catty [catapult] and got one of them on the lug.'

See ALL PAGGERED AND POOTLED, p. 115, *and also* BLETHERED, BUSHWHA, DIRT DEEN, JIGGERED, LAMPERED, MAGGLED

wack

a Liverpudlian (Liverpool)

If **fab** and **gear** were two of the terms that the Fab Four brought with them from 1960s Liverpool and placed swiftly within the national vocabulary, then **wack**, used in general (and often as a term of address) of a friend and specifically of a fellow Scouser, was not far behind. The word is a local abbreviation of **wacker**, meaning active – thus a 'wacker little fellow' – which in turn goes back to the standard English word wakeful.

wag, hop the wag

to play truant (London and Lancashire)

To **wag** or to **hop the wag** dates back to the mid-nineteenth century. It is included in the journalist and chronicler Henry Mayhew's 1861 study *London Labour & the London Poor*, where he also mentions **playing the wag**, an idiom which the *Oxford English Dictionary* sees as being linked to wag meaning 'a mischievous person', and thus 'playing the fool'.

Wagging can also be found in *Dombey & Son* by Charles Dickens, and early evidence suggests it was Londoners who started the practice. By the twentieth century, however, the word was common in the North, and it remains particularly used in Lancashire. As for its origin, the term may go back to a mid-nineteenth-century Cockney pronunciation of **vag**, a term for a vagrant.

See BUNKING AND PLUNKING, p. 192, *and also* BUNK OFF, DOG, MITCH, NICK OFF, PLAY HOOKEY, PLUNK, SAG, SKIDGE, SKIVE, TWAG

waken

(of a child) lively (North Midlands)

> **Waken** is probably an extended use of waken meaning 'awake', although the forms recorded, such **wakken** and **wacken**, strongly suggest that the influence of **wick** can be seen. One collector of Cheshire dialect at the end of the nineteenth century commented that the term 'rather implies that the lad has a spice of harmless mischief in him'.

> *See* TEARDOWN TEARAWAYS, p. 179, *and also* LISH, SKODADIDDLE, UNEASY, WICK, YAP

wean

baby, child (Scotland and northern England)

> **Wean** is a contraction of **wee ane** ('little one') into a single noun, with the earliest unambiguous example of it as a single word being in 1728. It is recorded everywhere where wee is a standard or at least well-known alternative to little. So it can be found throughout Scotland, in Northern Ireland and also in the northern part of England, but its epicentre is the south of Scotland. All the writers associated with southern Scotland, from Burns and Scott through Robert Louis Stevenson to James Kelman and Irvine Welsh, use the word as the standard term for a small child. The analogous **littl'un**, or **littlan**, is also found in much the same areas.

> *See* SMALL TALK, p. 228, *and also* BABBY, BAIRN, CHIEL

Small talk

Compared to our grandparents, babies and children have attracted only a handful of colloquial names. Maybe those who care for them are too busy to have time for neologism. There are, however, a number of slang terms that have arisen from specific contexts. **Sprog**, for example, originates in military slang, for it originally meant 'new recruit, trainee'. **Kid** is likely to have been in Old Scandinavian the word for a baby goat, as in the standard English today, brought to England by the Vikings. It was first used to refer to a human child in the London slang of the late seventeenth century. But on the whole, enduring local synonyms are hard to find, and are in the main restricted to Scotland and the north of England. Most have simple etymologies, being a variant pronunciation of a standard word (e.g. **babby**, **chiel**) or a self-explanatory term like **wean**. **Bairn** is by far the most noteworthy alternative, having been standard in Scotland and the far north of England for 600 years or more. But in pockets of Britain you can still hear **nipper**, **babe** and **ankle-biter** (borrowed from the US). Iona and Peter Opie's collection of the *Lore and Language of Schoolchildren* from the 1950s includes the wonderful observation that 'a chap who has got duck's disease is most often labelled "Tich" in a friendly manner, or "squirt" or "little squirt" in a less friendly manner. Alternatively: ankle biter, dolly mixture.'

See BABBY, BAIRN, CHIEL, WEAN

wedge

a lot of cash (London and UK-wide)

Relaunched into general use in the 1980s, **wedge** has been around as a piece of criminal slang for many centuries. Based on the actual lump or wedge of silver from which coins and plate are beaten out, it began by meaning silver coins in general, then added silver plate, which itself was melted back into wedges by criminal receivers, who were for a while known as wedges themselves. The modern use, doubtless reflecting inflation, conjures up a thick, chunky roll of banknotes, usually folded in half (and resembling a wedge); thus a large amount of money or wealth in general.

wet

to brew tea (the South-West)

Like many words now recorded in the South-West, **wet** formerly had a wider currency across the whole of the south of England. Indeed, at the end of the nineteenth century, a specific meaning for wetting the tea was found in Kent, defined as 'to pour a little boiling water on the tea; this is allowed to stand for a time before the teapot is filled up'. This wider southern use tallies with the word's use in, for example, H. G. Wells's novel *Kipps*, which is set, again, in Kent.

See KETTLE'S ON, p. 185, *and also* BIRLE, EMPT, HELL, MASH, MASK, SCALD, SOAK, TEEM

whim-wham

a trifling matter; a passing fad (Northamptonshire)

Some words just sound right, and **w(h)im-w(h)am**, meaning a 'trifle', 'nothing' or 'momentary fad', is surely among them; its peers, all synonyms, include **flim-flam**, **jim-jam** and **trim-tram**, and they too are applied to trivial or frivolous things. Whim-wham is further defined as 'a fanciful or fantastic object or idea'; 'an odd fancy', 'a child's toy', 'a snack or food' and 'a waterwheel', 'a weathercock' and 'a rattle to frighten away birds'. In other words, it is a multi-purpose word.

Whim-wham's origins remain mysterious, but there may be a connection to the old Norse word *hvima*, meaning 'to wander with the eyes as with the fugitive look of a frightened or silly person', and hvimsa, meaning 'to be taken aback or discomfited'. Thus it may be another of those words brought over by Britain's Scandinavian conquerors. Whatever the answer, whim-wham offers itself to a number of phrases: **all on the whim-wham** means 'shaking' or 'quivering' (used of something that has been insecurely fastened); to be **as contrary as a whim-wham** is to be very cross. **A whim-wham for a goose's bridle**, meanwhile, is something that April Fools are sent to look for, while **making a whim-wham to wind the sun up** is a way of side-stepping some child's query of 'What are you doing?' In the same vein, to be **making a whim-wham for a threshing-machine**, or **a whim-wham for waterwheels**, is to idle away one's time by doing nothing at all. The over-eager child can also be fobbed off by **making a whim-wham for a mustard-mill** or a **treacle-mill**.

whopper

an ostentatious idiot (Liverpool)

The verb **whop** means 'to thrash' or 'to defeat', and probably comes from its echoic sense of one object coming into abrupt contact with another. Taken figuratively it created the noun **whopper**, defined variously as 'a notably large object or person', 'a particularly unashamed lie', 'a painful fall' and in the plural, 'well-developed female breasts'. The figurative use is extended in Liverpool where the 'notably large' imagery has brought whopper to mean an 'ostentatious (and thus large) idiot'.

wick

alive, living (northern England); an active child (the North)

'You get on my **wick**' means, of course, 'you irritate me', and is a piece of (coarse) rhyming slang, even if the meaning does suggest that what is really suffering is our sense of self. There are no such buts about the northern use of **'wick** (with an apostrophe), which is an abbreviation of the standard quick, as in 'living or endowed with life'. **Quick** is linked to a wide range of European languages, whether Dutch, German (and all its older versions), Icelandic, Swedish and so on. Further back still one finds the Latin *vivus*, 'living', and ultimately the Sanskrit, the root-source of all Indo-European languages, *jīva*. So it is that in a 1970s edition of *Lancashire Life* we hear of 'Granny Martha Mosscrop, approaching her century and as wick as a flea'.

Wick is also, and importantly, the nearest thing to a predominant northern term for an active child, being recorded in Lancashire, Cumbria, Durham, and most parts of Yorkshire and Lincolnshire. Quick itself is recorded in this sense in Staffordshire.

See TEARDOWN TEARAWAYS, p. 179, *and also* LISH, SKOPADIDDLE, UNEASY, WAKEN, YAP

wisht as a winnard

ill; cold and hungry (Cornwall)

> To seem **wisht as a winnard** (or simply to **look like a winnard**) is a Cornish phrase meaning 'to appear either very ill, or very cold and hungry'. It might seem, for those not intimately aware of bird-life (and probably for them as well), a strange combination. **Wisht** is a wide-ranging and rather spooky negative, meaning variously unlucky, uncanny, eerie, awe-inspiring, horrible, mad, wild, sickly, haggard or white-faced. **Wishtness** is either witchcraft or, if personified, a ghost; the **wisht-hounds**, straight out of the nightmare cupboard, are spectral hounds, presumably of hell; **wishtful** means 'melancholy' and **wishtfulness** 'sadness' (not, surprisingly, related to wistfulness). Not much fun so far. To get our phrase we add the **winnard**, otherwise known as the redwing, *Turdus ilacus*. Quite why the hapless redwing, a relation of the thrush and blackbird, should be seen as a harbinger of sorrow or sickness is unknown: the probable reason is that the bird only appears in winter, a time of doom and gloom. A variant, meaning just the same, but a bit less sinister, is **mazed as a curlew**, a phrase that may in its turn refer to the bird's cry.

woollyback

an outsider (Liverpool)

> In Australia a **woolly** is a sheep, and in Liverpool, where **woollyback** means 'an outsider or non-local', (with the accent on a country-dweller and all the stereotypes that such a life implies) the sheep is still central to the image. Unflattering it may well be, but it is at least a kinder term than the synonymous **sheepshagger**, another Liverpool term for the hapless peasant, and well-known as the title of Niall Griffiths's novel of 2001. A similar term in Yorkshire for a non-local is **offcomeduns**, a variation of the term **offcomer**.

yap

(of a child) active; hungry (Scotland and the North)

A Scottish and northern word, **yap** originally, in the fourteenth century, meant 'nimble, active' and also 'cunning, shrewd'. Its meaning then passed into 'eager, ready' and by the eighteenth century in Scotland the eagerness was almost always for food: in other words, if you were yap you wanted your food, and quickly. An early eighteenth-century sermon by John Wyllie of Clackmannan informs us that 'young infants are very yap in the morning'. This sense has also been recorded in Northumberland.

See TEARDOWN TEARAWAYS, p. 179, *and also* LISH, SKOPADIDDLE, UNEASY, WAKEN, WICK. *See also* LEERY FOR LUNCH, p. 106, *and,* CLAMMED, CLEMT, HUNGERED, LEER/LEERY

yex, yesk

to belch, to hiccup (Scotland)

In Shropshire, a **yask** is the sound made by a violent effort to get rid of something stuck in your mouth. It is a variant on the Scottish **yesk** or **yex**, and all three words were born on account of their imitative sound.

Index

The book is organised in alphabetical order of dialect terms. The index only covers other local variants and spellings, locations, meanings and origins.